The Rules of the Game

The Rules of the Game

Selected Shorter Poems
1952-2008

by
Ludwig Zeller

Translated by A.F. Moritz

QUATTRO BOOKS

The publication of *The Rules of the Game* has been generously supported by the Canada Council for the Arts and the Ontario Arts Council.

We acknowledge the financial support of the Government of Canada, through the National Translation Program for Book Publishing for our translation activities.

Author's photograph: Joseph Sorrentino
Cover collage: "La eterna transformación" ("Permanent Transformation") by Ludwig Zeller
Cover design: Diane Mascherin
Editor: Allan Briesmaster
Typography: Grey Wolf Typography

Library and Archives Canada Cataloguing in Publication

Zeller, Ludwig,
    The rules of the game / Ludwig Zeller ; translated by
    A.F. Moritz.

Poems.

Issued also in electronic format.

ISBN 978-1-927443-19-4

I. Moritz, A. F.   II. Title.

PS8599.E45R85 2012   C861'.64   C2012-903879-2

Published by Quattro Books Inc.
382 College Street
Toronto, Ontario, M5T 1S8
www.quattrobooks.ca

Printed in Canada

Table of Contents

Introduction

THE POETRY OF THE Chilean, Ludwig Zeller, with its combination of baroque, romantic and modern elements, its experimental thrust toward the future, and its universal, classic preoccupations, is a unique fusion of Spanish, Spanish American, Surrealist and German Romantic currents. It's the fusion that should be emphasized, for Zeller's vision is the retort or alembic (one of his favourite images) in which such elements are mixed and transformed. The passionate and strenuous, not to say burnt and scarred, nature of this vision, which yet does not preclude humour, irony, idealism, love, beauty, and even a Horatian graciousness, stands out immediately in a glance over his work. This unified multifaceted attitude expressed in consummate verse leads Álvaro Mutis to place him in the "sainthood of poetry" with Blake, Hölderlin, Rimbaud, Georg Trakl, Henri Michaux and Robert Desnos. Like them, says Mutis, Zeller is a "predestined worker" who "must at every instant invent freedom, that paradise on earth which hostile humanity attacks at every instant"[1]—an assessment that appropriately implies the surrealist trinity of "poetry, freedom, and love," to which Zeller's work adheres.

Zeller was born in 1927 in the Atacama Desert of northern Chile, one of the world's most arid regions, in a village called Rio Loa after a nearby river, the only one in the area that makes it to the sea, if as a rivulet. His father, a German chemical engineer, had emigrated to South America and had married a daughter of the prominent Ocampo family. Zeller *pére* was head of the plant for manufacturing dynamite, used in Atacama mining operations, that gave the town its reason for being, and Mr. and Mrs. Zeller were the centre of society. The Zeller residence with its surrounding pepper trees planted by Zeller's father was a focal point of fiestas and served as a landscaping model to the local people, a tradition that Zeller and his companion Susana Wald continue today in their home near Oaxaca, Mexico.

13

Zeller is a poet of childhood. His first source is the eternal presence, joyous yet sometimes fearsome, of his early days with his parents and brothers and sisters, and its harsh, mysterious, brilliant setting. It is a "place absolutely crammed with mirages, a region I have never entirely left, not even for a second," he has said.[2] The parents provided a world in which the garden-ringed house harmonized with and protected against the landscape's beloved but scarcely endurable intensity. Within this setting, childhood experiences were a gradual introduction to strange realities. The taking apart of a clock on the sand to reveal its works and leaving it to lie disassembled. The folding of giant cardboard wheels, invented by Zeller's father, and setting them out in the desert in the afternoon, so they would blow away in the winds, disappearing, it seemed, forever into the flat empty distance, and then come rolling back with the opposite winds on the following day. The children would climb the pepper trees, or lean out on the balcony: in the evening to feel the stirring air and watch the sunset, and in the noontime heat to examine the vast mirages of flat water and of far-off objects: ships, for instance, and huge butterflies. At such hours, they were restricted to the house and balcony to prevent their becoming lost in the desert because of the mirages. But there were also explorations of the band of brothers and sisters along the riverbed and into the hills and cliffs, where sometimes a discovery was made: parts of an aboriginal skeleton in a cave, or perhaps a "demon-lament," as the local people called the prehispanic clay vessels that sometimes accompanied the ancient burials, and that emitted a haunting voice when blown into. Such scenes often recur in his poems and in his novel *Rio Loa: Station of Dreams* (1994).

Zeller was educated at a Jesuit high school at Antofagasta. Graduating at only 15, he entered the Jesuit order and was in seminary for four years, leaving on his own sudden decision. He went to the capital, Santiago, and began his higher education at the Instituto Pedagógico de la Universidad de Chile, the university's school of education. But his interests quickly migrated toward the city's vigorous, experimental literary and artistic life. He decided that the Pedagógico "seemed more like a place for training grade school teachers than a university."[3] Nor did his participation in the drawing and painting courses at Santiago's School of Fine Arts impress him favourably by comparison with the art he was learning and practicing on his own. Then, at the age of 21, he was struck with a life-threatening case of meningitis, from which he escaped with a memory that had been affected, another *ur-*experience often reflected in the poems and one which gives a peculiar, personal intensity to his employment of the pervasive term and theme of Spanish poetry, *el olvido*: the forgotten, forgottenness, oblivion. After his convalescence, he did not return to the university, eschewing further formal education in favour of taking his place in Santiago's flourishing, turbulent cultural world. Meaning to become a leading part of a new generation, Zeller at first defined himself in defiance to the Mandrágora surrealist group (1935-48), with its founding and core membership of Braulio Arenas, Jorge Cáceres, Teófilo Cid, and Enrique Gómez-Correa. Other prominent vanguard writers and artists of the time, some of them sympathetic to Mandrágora, include poets Rosamel del Valle and Humberto Diaz-Casanueva, Pablo de Rokha (the most famous Chilean antagonist of Neruda), and the painter Roberto Matta. All of these eventually became friends and associates of Zeller, some as the 1950s proceeded and some in the following decade.

Mandrágora, although it was exceptional in its surrealism and although it had formally disbanded just as Zeller arrived in Santiago, largely determined the cultural tone of the moment, and established surrealism as the country's advanced current. It had arisen at the time of the Spanish Civil War, when Chile, like Mexico, developed special ties to Republican Spain. The young writers who formed the group, oriented toward the European vanguard, adopted André Breton's position after his withdrawal of the Surrealist group from the French Communist Party that only complete freedom from political ideologies—artistic freedom, or rather, surrealist freedom—constituted a revolutionary path: "Jamais la liberté que pour la liberté."[4] As with the French Surrealists, this set the young Chileans off on a course of lusty, and painful, opposition to the institutionalized right and the church on one hand, and on the other the socialist opposition, increasingly dominated in Chile, as worldwide, by the Communist Party. The contention between big-party right and big-party left occupied the whole political and cultural scene, except for those who sat out, and, with Mandrágora's advent, these boisterous young poets, attacking both sides and attacked from both.

The ferment over the issues established in the late 1930s continued throughout the years of the Second World War and afterwards, and when Zeller arrived in Santiago in 1949 he plunged from his world of savage and innocent childhood into this second world of adult contention over power and the form of society. During the war, Mandrágora and its sympathizers continued to protest against the government, repressive convention, and institutionalized socialism, especially Communism, in favour of the attempt to encourage movements it considered properly revolutionary and to work in the independent and completely "other" form of surrealist creative vision. In 1944 the group's *bête noir* Neruda had been elected a senator, and in 1945 he had joined the Chilean Communist Party, later serving as publicist in the successful presidential campaign of Gabriel González Videla. When the latter went back on socialist promises and outlawed the Communists, Neruda published an open letter (1947) that resulted in issuance of a warrant for his arrest, and the famous episode of his months of hiding and his 1949 escape across the Andes into Argentina. In 1948, Mandrágora disbanded against this background of increasingly stable entrenchment of the right in government, and increasingly complete dominance of the disenfranchised left by Communism.

Zeller arrived on the scene with a harder attitude, seeing in politics itself the problem and the enemy. His work was resolute in spurning the issues as then defined and in its option for a purely creative approach. His radical rejection of political forms so false, in his opinion, as to have no hope of a good result was a disregard that had seemed theretofore impossible in the polarized atmosphere. He has described his 1950s in Santiago as "full and varied activity in literature, art, education and other experimental areas"[5] with special attention to "Spanish translation of the German Romantics" (Novalis, Jean Paul, Achim von Arnim, etc.), which he did in collaboration with his then wife, Wera. This resulted principally in his first book, *The Great Elegies of Hölderlin* (1950) and his series of lectures, "Historical Development of German Romanticism" (1951). During this period Zeller's first poems appeared in magazines and a series of limited editions that were later collected in his full-length books *Exodus and Other Solitudes* (1957) and *From the Source* (1961). In the early 1960s, too, Zeller made direct contact with the Paris surrealist group, "with Breton ... and with certain other people whose work interested me."[6] During this period, he also gave university lectures on contemporary literature, and formed many of his definitive literary associations. "I'd been in disagreement with the Mandrágora group for years," he has said, "chiefly because of the demands a difference in age makes, but now that the group had dissolved, I was friendly with all the people who had participated in it."[7]

No less productive in artistic fields, he brought his astonishing proficiency with the scissors, a childhood acquirement derived from folk art, to the making of intricate paper cut-out calligrams and abstract designs, and he combined this ability with his poetic vision to begin his historically important contribution to the characteristic surrealist art of collage. He made collages in contemporary materials, such as his collage portraits, but his main influence came in his revitalization of the old-engravings mode of collage associated with Dada and with Max Ernst. To this he brought an entirely new imagination, a new technical excellence, and a transforming idea: the elimination of pictorial background and the establishment of white space as contextless context, zone for the imagination's construction of worlds of splendour or disaster populated by his strange beings mixed of animal, machine, implement, cordage and drapery, and by free-floating flocks of spheres, mollusks, weapons, metal pieces—the sky-less and sea-less clouds and stars and fish and birds of a new universe. The resulting works combined abstraction with surrealist representationalism, and joined the crowded anarchy of Ernst's collage world to the foreboding stillness of de Chirico's painting.

Then, too, Zeller had become, at the age of only 24, an important animator of cultural life. The connections of friendship, collaboration and encouragement he established with the younger and more experimental artists, and the increasing notice given to his own work, led to his employment in 1951 as curator of the art gallery of the Chilean Ministry of Education and an additional, parallel position as the ministry's Advisor for the Plastic Arts, roles which he held until 1967. During these fifteen years he organized more than 200 exhibits and was crucial in providing an outlet and public recognition to advanced currents in Chilean art. In the mid-1950s he pushed his own experimentation farther, for instance producing large murals (about six feet by seven feet) in collage, and incorporating verbal elements: a 1957 mural-collage in contemporary materials included forty-eight "false proverbs." The activities that Zeller classes under "education" may include his curatorial activity and his work on German romanticism, but they must also take in his involvement with psychoanalysis and with the psychology of C.G. Jung. Characteristically, he absorbed the surrealist interest in madness but insisted upon not letting it remain a symbolic image based on distant realities or brief encounters. In 1962-64 he took yet another position, this one in the Centre for Anthropological Medicine at the University of Chile's School of Medicine. Here he had two roles: as an "assessor" in studies of verbal disintegration in schizophrenics, and as consultant on difficulties of communication between doctors and their patients. At the same time, he undertook a three-year experiment in the technique called "guided waking dream" under the Jungian analyst Dr. Helena Hoffmann. These activities and his increased immersion in Chilean surrealism greatly affected his poetry of the 1960s and 1970s.

Zeller and Wera eventually separated and Zeller found a new love in his companion ever since, Susana Wald, a painter and ceramicist. In 1968, the two founded Casa de la Luna, an art centre and drop-in house, also a magazine and independent publisher—a response to new circumstances, for 1967 saw the end of Zeller's employment at the Ministry of Education because of intense bureaucratic harassment under the Christian Democrat government then in power. This was a small incident in the increasing political contentiousness that would lead to the events of 1970-73: the election and presidency of the socialist-progressive Salvador Allende, the constant contestation of his mandate, mainly by the political right with support from the United States, and his death in the 1973 military coup d'état, resulting in a dictatorship under General Augusto Pinochet. In the late 1960s Zeller's position became increasingly difficult, since it was not accepted, except in a small artistic community, to be against both sides in the dominant socialist/reactionary debate, to be against the whole nature and form of the contest. Zeller continued to work as an independent curator and to publish his poetry. In 1968 he brought out his third and fourth books; his own imprint, Casa de la Luna, collaborating with Amigos de Arte, published the collection *The Rules of the Game*, and the major publisher Editorial Universitaria issued *The Pleasures of Oedipus*, an ironic montage-text of poems, apocryphal ancient quotations, and collages. He also mounted one final, landmark project, a comprehensive exhibit, "Surrealism in Chile." The year was 1970, the time of Allende's electoral campaign and victory, and the increasingly bitter, entrenched words and actions of the right from all its own seats of power and influence. "Surrealism in Chile," which opened before the election, was kept free of political innuendo and in this respect contradicted the polarized debate in which the two sides denied breathing-space to all but their adherents. After the exhibition, there was only the now completely polarized political landscape of

Chile as it had then become. Zeller found himself threatened, stripped of his living, constantly pressured to pledge the allegiance he refused, and existing in a suppressed, depleted artistic environment. In 1971, he and Wald determined to emigrate to Canada.

From then until 1993, Zeller lived in the Toronto area, first in a suburb, then in a neighbouring city, then downtown. Linguistically and socially cut off during these years, Zeller began meditating on his isolation and on the significance of his lifelong obsession with women and the theme of the feminine. The first four years after arrival in Canada produced his long poem, *Woman in Dream*, and a book on his isolation, which reflected it directly but also transformed it into a universal vision of exile in sixteen poems and sixteen related collages: *When the Animal Rises from the Deep the Head Explodes*. Zeller's early Toronto exile also resulted in more than 200 collages, and in the invention of a new collaborative form, the "mirage," in which Zeller contributed collage and Wald painting and drawing to a single surface.

Zeller's poetry of the late 1960s and the 1970s is unified despite the watershed of the move to the "antipodes" in 1971. Unity lies in the purer adherence to surrealism, only a contributing element in his work of the 1950s, whose originality had been its recapitulation of romanticism in a contemporary register, and whose attitude to surrealism had been partly a contention against the hard surrealism of Mandrágora, a contention the young Zeller had carried out by means of a return to various possibilities, surrealist ones but several others, found in the seminal Chilean vanguardist Vicente Huidobro. The poetry of the 1960s and 1970s increases the presence of formal, stylistic and thematic elements of surrealism in Zeller's work, but at the same time it recapitulates and intensifies the mythic figures found in the earliest poems. Relatively benign, edenic images of and prayers to the omnipresent feminine God transform into anguished pleas, hoarse and angry shouts, and a rediscovery of her as an almighty being who is, paradoxically, simply our sister upon earth, as much subject to time, chance, delusion and self-delusion, injury and disappointment as we ourselves are. Anna Balakian has well described this phase of his poetry as characterized by "powerful, sometimes eidetic, other times demonic imagery of minds wandering in the labyrinthine realms of roots and entrails, of man-made gadgets intertwined with nature's gargoyles, oozing with blood and mire: if there is honey and gold emerging out of his vision there is also coal, salt and rain that can taste of vinegar."[8]

Balakian comments that when Breton "declared man to be a definitive dreamer he was thinking of the exalting dream, greater than life in its pleasure producing capacity, idyllic, innocent, raising to sacred levels the meager reality of routine awareness" and states that "in temperament, Zeller and Breton are quite distinct," Zeller having reached, from the same point of departure, "entirely different skies" where "dreams can be nightmares coming after hours of insomnia; and they do not always liberate you from the reality of the waking state."[9] It would be accurate to say that Zeller expresses this hellish insight, but that his work balances it with its dialectical opposite: not the assurance of the transforming dream but the constant insistence upon the hope and quest for it. A Quixotic quest, ever renewed in the face of constant defeat. Somewhat submerged, except as prayer and question, in the work of the 1970s, this element resurfaced in the later poetry.

At Huron Street in Toronto, the Casa de la Luna of Santiago days were in part reconstituted. Every inch of the walls was covered with art that made a strenuous exotic contrast with its restrained North American context, including works by Wald and Zeller—ceramics, collages, paper cut-out calligrams, drawings, paintings, and "mirages"—and also paintings, photography, graphic art and sculpture by artist friends from around the world. Wald and Zeller established Oasis Press to publish poems and other texts by contemporary authors, including many of Zeller's Chilean contemporaries, now scattered or dead, such as Humberto Diaz-Casanueva, Rosamel del Valle, and Jorge Cáceres, as well as short books or chapbooks by new literary acquaintances. The family achieved a measure of security and a fund of associations when Susana became a professor of art at Sheridan College. In addition, Zeller and his works, poetic and graphic, began to come to the notice of Canadians and Americans. By 1973, he had had three one-man shows of collage in Toronto galleries, and throughout the decade this activity expanded: one-man and group shows in Toronto and several other Canadian locations, as well as in Chicago, in Caracas, Brussels, Paris, São Paulo, Lisbon, Bochum (Germany), London, Mexico City and elsewhere. In terms of his visibility in his adopted country, this activity culminated in a major 1979 exhibit at the Art Gallery of Hamilton (Ontario), "By Four Hands," which presented a retrospective of both his and Wald's work, as individuals and in collaboration. Simultaneously, Zeller's poetry was attracting the attention of literary people. At first his texts were not available in translation, so his initial appearances were in suites of photographically reproduced collages in the prominent Canadian literary magazines *The Malahat Review* and *The Tamarack Review*. In 1975, *Kayak* (an influential American "little magazine" with an international bent) published *Dream Woman* as a small book in a translation by Fernando Alegría and *Kayak* founder and editor George Hitchcock. Later the same year Zeller himself issued the poem as *Woman in Dream* from Oasis in matching volumes, one containing the Spanish and one the English translation by Estela Lorca. Then, the Canadian writers John Robert Colombo and Thérèse Dulac made excellent translations of *When the Animal Rises from the Deep the Head Explodes* in English and French, allowing this book to be published in 1976 in a trilingual edition. This activity culminated in a major volume, *Ludwig Zeller in the Country of the Antipodes*, which offered English translations of all his published poems from *The Rules of the Game* to three new long poems, and which appeared in 1979, the same year as "By Four Hands."

This was the high point of Zeller's public presence in Canada. He became the subject of feature articles, interviews and reviews in national periodicals and newspapers, as well as commentaries in literary and art magazines. Attention was magnified by the country's awareness that his art was increasingly exhibited abroad, that his poetry and collages were being accorded essays and book chapters by José Miguel Oviedo, Anna Balakian, Arturo Schwarz and others. In the largely nationalist Canadian literary context, his presence buttressed the work of certain established Canadian writers with internationalist leanings, and encouraged the development of younger ones who eventually created Canadian poetry's strong present-day strain of renewed, if ironic and hip, surrealism and dada. But by the mid-1980s Zeller was again private stock for a few, and in 1986 when he exhibited at the XLII Venice Biennale, and in 1987 when he was the featured poet of the Rotterdam International Poetry Festival, these honors went without printed notice in Canada.

In the late 1980s, Mexican cultural figures increasingly encouraged Zeller and Wald to locate in their country, and several events cemented the decision: encounters around Zeller's participation in a Wolfgang Paalen tribute exhibition at the Museo Carrillo Gil in Mexico City, the Mexican publication (1988; 2nd ed. 1993) of his selected poems *Save Poetry Burn the Bridges*, and an invitation from the municipal president of Oaxaca to reside in that city and produce publications for its cultural, anthropological and historical agencies. By 1988 Zeller was living three months of each year in Oaxaca, and Wald was spending her winters there, where, turned architect, she was designing their unique house, two studios joined by a common area, on a hilltop in San Andrés Huayapan, a village overlooking the city. In 1991, Zeller was the featured artist and writer of the Guadalajara Book Fair, with a major retrospective exhibit of both publications and artworks, and an accompanying book-length catalogue, *Zeller Free Dream*. Since 1994, when Wald retired from her professorship at Sheridan College, the couple has lived in Oaxaca and Huayapan, painting, writing and making collages and mirages. In 1994 Zeller published a second selected volume, this one concentrating on erotic poems, *To Saw the Belovèd to Pieces When Necessary*. In 1996 appeared his collected poems, *The Gears of Enchantment*; in 2003, at the commissioning of the University of Michoacán, a highly unusual travelogue, 101 poems under the title *The Enthrallment of Mexico*; and more recently two further Mexican volumes. Exile from Chile also began to be eased; renewed attention there resulted in his 2007 invitation to be the featured poet and the subject of the annual Chile Poetry Festival, and in the simultaneous award of a doctorate *honoris causa* by the University of Chile. Thus at 80 he became an honorary professor of the university in a ceremony in the same building where fifty-seven years earlier he had delivered his lecture courses. Now he was hailed by young poets as "the last surrealist," and asked for talks, interviews and readings as a rare surviving link to a crucial strand of Chilean culture that had been nearly cut by the years of the Pinochet dictatorship. As a result, Chile has recently produced a series of publications by and about Zeller, including a large selected poems and collages, an edition of his novel *Rio Loa, Station of Dreams*, and a major overview of his career, *Ludwig Zeller: The Architecture of the Writer*.

Zeller's poetry had, during the mid-to-late 1980s, developed a third phase. The fiery, scarred and vertiginous aspect of his perception remained, but tended to remove itself from style and exist primarily as subject matter and image, while the style returned to a combination of the Golden Age Spanish grace and the German Romantic lyrical plangency of Zeller's earliest period. Further, the style itself now considered, as well as participating in and suffering, the human dilemma. In this way, it freed itself for more complete expressions of compassion, hope, and the undying search. The lexical and argumentative content of the poem turned on itself and examined this dialectic of suffering and wisdom that had now arisen between subject matter and manner. The late poems give concentrated expression to the continual alternation in humankind of hope and despair, energy and ennui, and insist upon converging these opposites, seeing them not only as peaks and troughs of a curve but as superimposed realities which in fact are one. Zeller thus reinvigorated the theme of *ilusión*, a word with a terminological status in Spanish poetic tradition, denoting the identity of hope and illusion, the dual fact that imagination does create an ideal reality but that, at the same time, all our dreams of good are imaginative projections.

Jacques Ellul, interpreting the poetry of *Ecclesiastes*, describes its poet's vision in terms that might be a reading of Zeller's late poetry: his "is not the vain harangue of someone who is by nature a pessimist... He tries to make intelligible the secret that the wise person should receive... But at every turn the author rams up against the same wall: all his experience, searching, and reflection lead to the same conclusion: either there is no wisdom, and everything is vapid, in which case the search for the secret of the universe is chasing after wind. Or else wisdom exists but cannot be communicated, in which case all is vanity, since nothing has meaning—except for knowing that there is a meaning we search for in vain."[10] Compare the end of "Monte Albán, Sacred Mountain," in which Zeller paraphrases pre-Columbian poetry:

We decorate in stone and are unmade in dust.
As the poet said, the quetzal's feathers are minuscule petals,
They move us, but no one knows what inwardly they are.
Perhaps the Life Giver is dreaming in us. But silence falls.

Yet the "trying to make intelligible the secret," and compassionate fellowship with humans, stuck with this quest and indomitably committed to it too, are equally present in his verse, the contradiction being surpassed in a strange though ancient vision of futility identical to triumph, extinction identical to endless love:

...we're on our way to celebrate
Poetry on the other side, near the heart where all those
    absences,
Wounds and wandering flames are quenched.

The paradoxical human fusion of pettiness and grandeur, delusion and imagination, extinction and exaltation exists because of a gift from beyond our possibilities and comprehension: "life, which is scarcely a breath and is eternal."

Notes

A longer version of this essay appeared in Spanish as the introduction to *Ludwig Zeller, arquitectura del escritor,* ed. Hernán Ortega Parada (Santiago de Chile: Editorial Cuarto Propio, 2009), 11-23.

1. Álvaro Mutis, "*Introducción: Ludwig Zeller o el espejo en entredicho*" in *Ludwig Zeller, Salvar la poesía quemar las naves* (Mexico City: Fondo de Cultura Económica, 1988; 2nd ed. 1991), 7

2. Alex Zisman, "An Interview with Ludwig Zeller," trans. Dallas Galvin, Review 21/22 (Fall/Winter 1977), 167-71; 167

3. Ibid., 167

4. *Clair de terre (précédé de Mont de Piété, suivi de Le Revolver à cheveux blancs et de L'air de l'eau)* (Paris: Éditions Gallimard, 1966); 110 (from "Non-lieu," 1932).

5. *Zeller Sueño Libre / Zeller Free Dream* (Oakville, New York, London: Mosaic Press, 1991); book produced as a catalogue to accompany the exhibition of the same name constituting Zeller's presence as featured author and artist of the 1991 Guadalajara Book Fair; 36

6. Zisman, 171

7. Zisman, 171

8. Anna Balakian, "The Surrealist Optic of Ludwig Zeller," *Review* 21/22 (Fall/Winter 1977), 161-65; 161

9. Ibid., 161-62

10. Jacques Ellul, *Reason for Being: A Meditation on Ecclesiastes*, tr. Joyce Main Hanks (Grand Rapids: William B. Eerdmans Publishing Company, 1990), 58

THE POEMS

Childhood's House

to my sister Kunigunde

Sometimes I wake and someone's shouting in the dark,
something flutters in closed graves, something whitens;
then doors open and I go down into shadow
after the phantom who watches over dreams.

O house, insane virgin, rooms I loved in childhood,
tell me how you grew used to yesterday. Does night
still make you afraid? Do you still sob when a wind runs
along your balconies, so loud that you can't hear?

I remember when you lifted your sad head,
like my mother looking out at the desert dust,
because happiness dies before it arrives, and the one joy—
the pleasure we take in fading—cuts like the thorn
of a dried thistle: nothing is forgotten, not ever,
the way an inscription in sand, constantly erased,
always rises again in the heart in the shape of pain.

Alone, sorry, deserted—house, do you remember?
When the day and hope, like hurrying travelers,
had passed us by, shadows arrived, the sun stained
your windows with blood and terror came or sometimes
the sick delight of a solitary looking at the moon.

Closed doors that spied on me like eyes,
putrefying beings that hung over my sleep and erased
footfalls in streets without end where I walked screaming...
tell me, do your doors still complain, do your wings still spread,
are you still calling me, looking toward the desert
where I'm lost? I feel treetops swaying
in my childhood but see only leaves pitilessly burnt,
an endless plume of smoke and a cry spinning,
struck and broken by unappeasable lights.

The Elements

In every sound the elements are heard,
fire...earth...air...water...
essences of life, faint shadows of the soul.

—The Delphic Oracle

Fire

You, skin of burning coals, interrogator,
turn to me, tell me, spin the salt syllables,
the mystery ghosts, of the fever breathing its memory
into my ears. Images made of blood.

I've seen you and I've waited for you
the night long. Resonance, word, prince of light,
you lit your campfires far above. Flame-woman, arrow
shot from the vast black stone, you ate
the ancient suns of worn-out seeing and I see you
hidden in a thousand bodies, an eternal moving-onward.
Faces, tongues, colours, time of the storm.
Metals tearing through flesh.
                              Outbreaks, flashes.
Are we plowing through the ash of minds yet to be born?

Warden of fever, lady, unravel your dream.
Watching the wells, a salamander stirs. You burnished wing,
you fire. Unmoved pupil of the eye of god.

Earth

Mother, provisioner of life, I spill my voice out to you
and bow down: makeress, through you the invisible
is real. Bodies, skin streaked with light, animals
loping in the sunset. O silent one.

Sphinx, you who put the question to night,
eternal outcry, oozing clay and kneading of the clay.
Dizzied and dizzying flesh, gust of life,
being half glimpsed in dreams... Once, long ago,
stretched out beneath a tree, you waited for a breeze.
You fulfilled yourself in many bodies: gilded fruits,
water jars, valleys where the Powers and Dominions were born,
enchanted seeds, mysterious and thirsty...

To you we return and unmake ourselves like flowers,
burnt by a sun named nostalgia. Mother of constant birth.
Stone carved with ciphers. Song. Our blood's harvest.
Golden springtime... Memory of a woman
stretched out beneath a tree, waiting for a breeze...

Air

Invisible lute. Diamond of breezes and breaths.
Who tears her fingers through your strings?
Who calls to you in silence? Who listens to you?

Melodies cross distances in a soul,
a pilgrim is nearing the fountains. Blades!
Scales! Dust! Semblances that turn
at the beckoning of a wing from another space,
a presentiment the colour of blue sky.

The light, that guest who waits to be thirsty,
to be craving—is it asleep in you? A tide
rises to you who are all one burning lip.
Silent lament of a drifting cloud.

Angel veiling the face of an adored body.

Water

What sands swallowed my days, my life? I search,
I comb through the dust in my chest, illusion of a body,
ash of light, the face of a dream,
the awakening of thirst...

        Spring bubbling up from memory,
you, murmur, soul of water, essence of life,
mysterious current that engrossed my childhood, song
of a woman straying in the desert—toward what?
I sense you eternally, pure, winged, crystal
tears of wanting. Lips moving. Unmovable love.
Sea of freedom, sky-earth, heaven-earth, wandering
mirror in which we enchant ourselves—far away,
lost and alone—always I feel you crying out,
in love, tenacious on the shore,
slave of the moon, mourner...

I wait here for your messengers from the sky.
        Pass by this way, as you used to,
Dream, serpent of living waters. Awaken the heart
beneath this soil. Will those messengers ever come back?
Samaritans, let's forget our water jars, put them down!
Can't you hear? A woman is crying at the well,
water is falling on the star of fever.

A Demon-Lament

Talk to me—who are you? What past have you come back from
to blow through my life? Who grew you, crying,
out of burnt earth; what loneliness, what breath
polished you from within like the scar over a burn,
what secreted desire do you mutter, demon,
in the night of fever, of ourselves?

Do you know the thirst that drinks us and the dust
that falls and keeps falling over life? Have you seen,
have you seen how pain scatters and sows
its salt in the days, have you felt how time
strikes, how being withers under its wings,
its predestined screeching up above us?

Do you vibrate, hard form, cold muteness, silence,
or are you only the stone in which I'll finally
rest my blood? I keep night watch. I hear you crying.
There are things that no longer exist in words,
beaches where our eyes can't see, burnt out
by the sun, turned to undying and unliving vision.

Divinity, let humans know what days mean. I love
your lip that spills, that breathes into me, Holy One,
the forms of life, I love the voice that never breaks off.
I want to be a flame in the ebb and wash of its breath,
an echo in that head from which dreams flow,
a wing's pulse in those veins where the sea beats.

The Acrobats

Like waters that quiet themselves around their centre,
the crowd's mutterings go out, all eyes fix once again
on lights in a striped sky, azure and yellow. What music
did they play? I try to remember. And then the image
leaps, full of sun and the thunder of drums.

Ladies and gentlemen, look! I hear from the mirror.
Behold their net like days, their rope a serpent,
life like a wing, the air an ocean
with singing foam, its voices the lightning bolts,
its storm the faces of those watchers over there.

Next I see her—timid as if she doesn't know how to sing—
lowering a thread into the depths of her mouth.
And that One who calls distantly in the Tree of Life:
his question lingers like a knife thrown
toward the skies, skies empty of birds. The acrobats

leap up a wall, their shadows fly, they fall
head first with a hubbub that stretches and twists
like a howl in a labyrinth; and the air holds them up,
father to son, woman to man, strange planets
above the plain of faces.

The game keeps repeating itself and they are insects
under the huge sheaf of rays: woman and her death, the chain,
and the tower that stands on one foot, keeping its balance
with a finger: then it climbs the final steps,
looks up and answers the sun's call one more time.

Traveler, you who pass by, a burning coal
before your eyes, talk to the tide, twirl the talismans,
the ropes that carry a sleepwalker to the wall
of his childhood, naked, unafraid, while far away
bonfires are consuming wings, consuming his days.

And he leaps up from his own depths, he breaks
the multicoloured mirror and arcs shouting through the air,
trembling toward a hand that holds his lifelines: the road,
the rope he picks up again, fastened
to a harpoon he takes now and clenches between his teeth.

...far down beneath him, men and women, the shock of the sea.

A Dove Dreamed

like days passing over the waters
a shadow of wings foam of the sky
flocks return to an invisible sea
seething wakes in the palms of your hands
you listen as those birds migrate
beating against mirrors

I see the ancient enigmatic bird renewed
in a verb whose flames cover the surface of things

hard light your gaze is reborn to the depths

then grant me bird-song your eternal leaves
your secret plumage that lives with dreams
in impossible spaces in quivering petals
where night nests and its eyes are
a black sky streaked with meteors

there it calls and waits the rain must be coming
to the dry carved lips the vertiginous face

so in some the remorseful light lives still
that I find on the inside of my eyelids

the foam that never comes back since silence fell

An Unbelievable Patient

"I was sitting there for a thousand years
Unable to wake, or sleep, or die,
My eyes turned downward in the bottom of a glass...
So tired... I would like to..."

I advise you
To think of nothing, float as the rivers do inside your skin,
Stretch out, let your limbs relax on the table,
Be only a formless mass without limits
Like a sandbag that laments, that mourns its twilight.

Now listen carefully:
     Close your eyes, try to open
The doors... Where are we? Answer.
Where are we?

               (Silence)
In the depths:
"I'm blind and dumb, now I can't even hear you...
My bones are eroding in the air..."
               (Silence)

Remember:
     If you come back, you'll always have a home here.
Here is your mirror, the chart with all your data.

I stumble out, I bow to excuse myself. I read
On the inside of my eyelids: "Box of Torture." The corroded
Mirror-silver lets nothing more be seen.
                              O search,
Search for me along the thread of blood.

To the One Who Watches Will Everything Be Revealed

Wind breathes in the steep vertical solitudes
Where birds that constantly open the veins of night
Strike and light their phosphorus heads on a knife-edge.

Behind my burned out eyes one image endures:
Ants devouring her incunabular nipple.
Thorns don't hurt here, they float on nothingness,
We fly in circles and her skin throbs and speaks to us.

"Nobody answers, sir, there's no such number, the wires
Have been cut, you can't hear anything, wake up to another
Dream in another place." The dove isn't coming back,
Ashes grow quiet in the courtyards of the Ark.

The Game of Truths

The claws as they extended joined the flame.
From the lip to the knives a single question goes.
Undressing in the sun, water lets her skin fall,
The birds describe the hollows of her shoulders.

In the mouth of the deep I hear beehives moaning,
Monsoons, high waves in the hair of fright. You laugh
Like the rains, you open yourself into the cold
Scissors of an animal behind its fangs.

I come down a stair, cry, cut, open the closed
Doors of dream. Do you renew your toys with the years?

Wealth To Count

I dream that I'm dreaming, I lean out on balconies
And it's the earth howling up there in the night sky.
We are traveling by foot across mute scars on the moon
To a cackling of Gorgons, the rulers here.

What am I doing in this place? Why does my scream
Cut their throats? Blindly groping, they twist their heads,
Clocks that leap broken to pieces on the ground—from each one
A thread winds into the skein of all knots: the blood.

Years pass, she smiles, the talking head without body,
The adored one who was my life. I want to force those walls
At flame point, open those two legs, those cruel parting
Lips of the embers of salt, of boredom's metals.

No water here. When I wake up I see their boiling scales
Scattered by a breath but I can't see you. In other lights
Feathers flow past like tongues. Your gaze is a caress
Of knives. To leave the labyrinth, to enter it, are one.

If She Came Back

Groping, she questions me. I see her on the roads.
Without unfolding her arms, she displays her fabulous merchandise.
Let's repeat, let's simulate, her voices: would we want to cease
Dreaming larvae like ladies with automatic teeth?

I remember you, oh Sublime (Habakkuk 2:11).
Contemplating the navel, her stones bored me.
It's scarcely possible her crows will sing. I give them back.
Let syringes prick them and they'll bellow patiently.
Do their cages, already sitting at the lowest depth,
Have floors that are mouths of bottomless wells?

Landscape for the Blind

I no longer recall when I withdrew from those wounds.
I shout in the dark, with my head I probe and delve
Into a wall, the years go on multiplying their swarm.
I don't know if I'm awake, if it's milk or vinegar they give me.

I open my fingertips into claws but they keep growing
Longer till they reach where her voices pulse and creak.
She will return with the rain. I've swallowed my tongue.
The globes, set aspin, are adjusting their accounts.

Where are we, groping, looking for a road to take us
Under the sun, past stumps of limbs and angry inscriptions,
Making our way through burnt ice, thrusting live coals
Into our eyes. Sweetly our glances lick each other.

What do you see? I see you gasp like a fish in another air.
What do you see? Only a desert of mirrors and the knife.
What do you see? My root torn from the feathers of your bowels.
What do you see? I can't see. I only feel you will come.

To Understand Is Not To Know

Day after day I wait.
At last they come. They ask me the names
Of forgotten beings with my own face
Who wither, shave, classify the world
And keep rising up.
I don't understand what for.

Night after night I dream you as two halves
Closed over me like the lips of the insect machine
That chews the numbers, pants in the scales
And leaps and suddenly is blood clotted on my pillow.
Purely blind, thick, rootless, in the light
The waters are crying.
I don't understand what for.

It's late. Tired now, the clock hands shatter,
And it seems to me we'll never reach anywhere.
Why so many flames, so much burnt pulp,
And that child who pastures his worms on arid knifeblades?
Why so many eyes? Why weren't we allowed to sound
The well in the antheap palace? Why does the dream
Dream itself, repeat itself in each nativity with its toys?
What for? Belovèd, answer me. What for?

With backs turned to our direction, we shoot along the rails
Unlamenting. A garden of rodent drills is waiting for me.
Hurled forward, in the airlessness, I wake up, sleep,
And wake again. I hear a knife in the distance.
A voice answers me from every shred:
Your doubts—rejected. To understand is not to know.

On the Waters

On the waters I watch my line oscillate
But I don't want to see what's there in the depths.
I warm a talking pebble in my hand,
And at night, roots grow by shrieks.

You, traveler passing by. My pupil pins you with its needles.
Speak to me, I've heard you coming up from dreams.
For you I have a little thrush that feeds only on eyes.
If you no longer remember who I am, then guess...

Your name
Was Anguioser, Ambrosia, Antadares, Ariadne.
Ants with pointed nipples carried madness.
If I move, the embers under my eyelids hurt.

The Locket of the Brontë Sisters

This is the locket
The Brontë sisters owned. I found it there in the dust,
Between the dry rails of the very station
Where they once waited for their impossible lover.

Their dresses had so many petals
That in admiring the pattern of the cloth life passed;
They smiled at each other glancing sidelong like someone
Who bites at a hard, mysterious secret...

Maybe none of it exists, maybe I alone
Hold the keys, the leaves of that time, but I am
Mute before them just as in childhood and I don't understand
Why no one comes, no one, no one will ever come.

In the Erotic Machine

Everything in that sphere was clear like water,
Sweet as the bee-swarm in the erotic machine.
He spun and spun till, finding spiral shells,
He turned them on their backs and put their vertebrae in order;
Later, he shut off the air, slowly sewed her lips together
To seal in the screams, and watched.

        What did you watch? My time
In the alembics, the sweet, the lascivious turbulence
Of listening with my eyes until I bleed insomnia
And see the sole image, ritual of the labyrinth
Where God tries on his new bodies.

Near the Burning Wheel

The crows made their nest near the burning wheel.
In a spiral they descended to drink from the bone.
Where can my mother be? Among the trees,
The tongue hears her honeycombs opening.

A cross whirls and the sharp edges
Of its teeth cut the onion on my back.
How sweet that root is. Here it's the cup where tears
Well up, there it's the twitching cup of claws.

Now that my feet are broken, I hear a knife
Like a curse. Where? And moving toward where?
The lamb bleats and bleats in a rain of blood.
A key opens its eyes, the road its wounds.

Year of the Quiet Sun

Years, quiet of time. On sweet terraces
Of the total season, almonds fall
From my pocket, bees deafen the sun.

Memory of Childhood

I found myself in a harbour with a sack
Of salt on my shoulders. There was no one there
And, walking past the old jetties, by the water I came
To that column of burning ceramic used for mooring
The ship that descends on its sails of feathers
Toward the open sea.

That's all I remember. It was
A long time ago. Today I drink through a crystal
That is deafened by the threads of the lamp.
Her words are roads of milk. She measures
My temples and, groping in the dark, keeps tracing by numbers
The image on the glass, hypnotized by a likeness, unaware
That wheels now move her tongue
And they've lowered their grapples into the sea forever.

Elsewhere, outside all this, people are sleeping and their dreams
Float in the ancient ships of the fog. Am I here
Or not? Someone smiles at the torture it is to be
Only what the seas drag to other beaches
Where naked bodies, remnants of shipwreck,
Move between sheets of sweetness and awaken.

Triumph of Oedipus

It's all finished. I hear them
Tying my arms in knots, and nails scraping
My eye sockets, where once the sun made its nest.

Why should I drink? Why do threads
Drag themselves from that well, there, in childhood?

A few more moons and you will no longer see me,
I will have come into the Kingdom. At the vinegar,
The thorns open slightly, but my memories never.

When the Animal Rises from the Deep the Head Explodes

Today come the ghosts and across a table that swirls
I see flowers grow beneath the parched crying
Of an eye that from the centre of a plate
Watches the jar filled with scorpions in oil.

Suddenly the days closed. Huge leaves grew
Like the pelts of leopards in ambush, they asked me
My name in Aramaic, they broke my bottles of frozen
Lightning, remnants of a love polished by the sea.

Surely he's one too many, they said. The clock
Mismanaged its gears, its pulleys moved in reverse
And I wander, a warm-blooded being, among animals
Along the roads, and champ my bit, loneliness.

Has the sun gone out, I ask. The children cry
And from the four quarters I hear bubbles rise and burst,
Without truce licking the planks, the marinated splinters
Of the Ark's hull. Under a fever-pall an ember smolders.

I don't want to see the guitar break,
I don't want to see, rising in the pot,
The eye with claws that asks yet again
If two and two are four, if the waters have truly boiled.

Dear ones, where are we? The sands of insomnia are rising.
Let's gather up these toys of terror, light a fuse to blast
The moon in two, and wait a thousand years... My squid,
My mother in her cloud of ink, suddenly starts sobbing.

Captain Cook's Last Port

Examining without pincers the rocks of his mind,
He thinks he sees the strange new lands again
And his ship and the green clay urns where blood screamed
In the skin of women hidden, sealed in them and forgotten.

But who is remembering? No way out. And the wind
Will never blow in these shrouds and stays, he's alone
And there's no one anymore on the deck where years ago
Captives drenched with rain, terror and rust
Sang in their jargon of shrieks like burning liquor
He wishes he could hear again today.

At last, though, he understands he's never left
This prison, and the adventure of exploring
Earth's four corners with their boiling dust
Was nothing but a legend told by drunken sailors.

Pride tempts him and his face grows cold
To all tenderness as, leaning on his stick,
He contemplates the secret he's kept for years, his dish
Of tears that were torrents once and wrecked him
In this maternal bay.

                      He looks at the burnt bones
That once he crossed singing or cursing, the wind beating
At last in the rigging like a wing and the lying road
That invites him to set out with the many others who now are
Crossing the map of his dreams, and he asks himself "Where?"
And there's silence, and he grows so hoarse with screaming he
        becomes
The lament of wanderers dragged by the tides
To the abyss without bottom and forever.

To Saw the Belovèd to Pieces When Necessary

Under the edges of the knife she feels
The moon's wheel, creaking in the mirror,
She thinks she is dreaming and she hears how, slit by slit,
The endless spiral of torture grows in her body.

They watch her with love and wait, standing
In the deafening rain: let the hand clenched there in the depths
Pull up the tips of dream with its hook;
And from the worm's putrefaction
May the exact butterfly fly away.

But nothing matters now and under the burning ray,
Its turnings and turnings, whirlwinds with a single centre,
At times I hear someone cry out, I wake up
And am looking at the same image, the torturer
Who is also the wounds, because I don't know
If it's water falling from above, if I just once will reach
The globe that the wind drags along, if we'll make it through
Or the night's valves will suddenly snap shut.

Then I get up and with no eyes I can see the knife
That someone has left here, pressed into my hand,
And the wheels, seeds of another sun, whirling in my memory
Slicing my loved one into hosts for me.

Louis Wain and the Cats

First all the doors must be bricked up,
The exits filled in or paved over, and all windows broken
That could reflect those eyes. Speak softly.
More softly still...
                Is Wain there, dreaming?

Stretched out on the sofa, castaway in a desert
Where the noises of infinite clocks explode,
He defends himself and image after image
Ends in threads of the fever that springs
On the sword-points of the eyes of cats.

Are they here or not? "Is there by any chance
A single one of us who is awake?" I hear screaming
And in the tearing apart of skin already burnt
By lightning the screams become unbearable.

Through his broken eyes he sees crystals fall
Inward inside him, flames consume him
And leap from his fingertips turned to claws, to nails.
What do they want, those cats, those eyes...?

But this day closes forever and horror
Geometrically multiplies his insomnia of a thousand nights.
Sleep no more. Why are the eighteen cats
Of my friend sinking in a mirror? Why is blood
Running on the window panes?
                  Is Wain there, dreaming?

Bad Habits

Each person keeps feeding his vices till the storm
Drags him like a herring
To a vat of salt. From there the body does not escape
Unless resplendently, clean of the skin
For which it burned—and then its step is light when,
Scarcely grazing objects, it pours itself into the glass
Of beating veins and the wet branches
No longer recognize it except for its light that traces the lines
Of the perfect belovèd.

There she will be dreaming,
Disguised as of old on a balcony of dust
The wind has blown away. "Why are you here,
Since moons never return and all the days we've counted
Are dice randomly thrown..."
And at once I feel the sea
Break on warm marble rocks, unspeaking wounds.

Who is it I keep waiting for, who, when my eyes already
Have cracked the walls and shelled them off? Rust falls,
It falls and I'm pulled into the deep by hooks, I'm hung
On a wire that someone moves to the mercy of his knives.

In the Land of the Antipodes

From the other side of my skin those enraged birds
Are calling me. Destroyed by love, they initiate
Grand gestures, ask questions and peck blindly,
Their warm feathers burning in the mirrors.

There's no captain to cut the quietude of the waters.
Pincers twist, adjusting my wounds: here was the point,
The mark, of those magnetic lips—the tide
Nailing us here, tattooing us with fire.

One head sleeps and the other keeps watch
Submerged in wine. I try to speak and time
Rains blood into the retorts. I shout out and wake up
And find myself lying on thorns. Who knows

If I'm here, if I've arrived? Suddenly the wind
Whirls the scales and in an eternal back-and-forth
I'm playing in my childhood, an old man
Surrounded by cybernetic hens.

Poetry and Truth

Sick and tired of proverbs, leaning back on a knot
That grows as a root from his body,
He watches the passing days, fragments of window pane
That render the sun for all its bellowing mute.

Pegged into his skeleton, a great tattooed
Sea hook raises its head, a grapple from the deep,
Without peace, solely of the waters, a Face
That is his face, that he looks at and does not know.

Astray in smoke, following a thread, a seam
Of coal, he remembers how light broke in two
Distinct worlds: over Ranu Raraku the sphinx
Changed its plumage, the torment of stones risen
From the depths, enigma-heads worn down by the sea
With its fixed gaze, the old engraving that now mildews
In his hand, and before it the flower of lava, his question.

Ontological Distraction

Life is only a tube without remedy.
Entering gives everyone the right to view the injustice,
Close it in his fist like a white-hot ember
And scream, tortured by its edges, or throw it
Like a burning spear into the cursed fabric
The spider keeps weaving over the other entrance
                              which is a dream that
Life is only a tube without remedy.

The Sphinx in Toronto

...And for this I walked more than forty years,
Bumping into furniture, breaking my bones on the edges
Of all the walls that, with their lidless eyes,
Have no water, only thirsty carbon, only ashes,
Dust that carries us along...
                              And the wind there in my childhood
Or here the gusts that shave my face with their cold
Stares, and walking, and asking myself where, while someone
Sews an unknown sentence into my back.

How many years. The masks keep being repeated
In the heart of a bonfire burning the last bees;
On the balcony my mother's ringlets moved in the wind—
Were we children today, yesterday...ever? The ciphers
Keep being repeated on the drumhead of foreign tongues,
The way someone looks at his palm, at a star growing there
Surrounded by shrieks and cawings—the star that will rise,
Cut through the azure and be a bird.

And now I'm here, naked before the godless,
Insolent Sphinx, like a man who asks himself
For the story of a disaster lost in the Latin
Of Pliny the Younger, who matter-of-factly described
His escape from the black flood that cascaded
Up from the depths. "I didn't see Vesuvius," he wrote,
"But a scar of fire and the fall of a total night.

The sun went out and, indifferent, I read some Livy,
Because that's how it is, life and its true cost, our arrogance."
And we cut a tunnel, another, and another, and in all of them
I find only stations of my mind, fragments of what I've lived,
Bodies in which once, alone, I was the soul.

But now I'm here. Three years are enough for the sun
To change its outer rind again and shine before humans
Like the serpent's egg. Lascivious fire is all around,
Memory that persists in each woman who used to be a chimera,
Her black shoes in the sand, and blue smoke singing
In her glance...

       But didn't I always foresee this? And am I safe now?
In the eyes here I see torment...a bouquet of falling tears.
Outside the ocean ramps. Inside the wind murmurs.
Could it be that I've arrived? That I've woken up?

Gradiva Passing

Like someone groping who hears the thunder
Of a remote past, she watches wreckage clash on the sand
And moves with the knife-edge dissecting the hive,
A bonfire now, besieged by insects.
Among the ruins other elytra call.

Then in the embers she examines lost ages, petrified horizons,
And eagerly licks the almond's secret folds,
Hearing a desire grow in her, deep as the deepest burn,
To go farther into the hieroglyph, which has started to glow,
And have no sackcloth, feathers or nails, but be solely lips:
From the real to the invisible falls the torrent with no end,
The flaming skin.

Our Sorrows

Old photographs hung on my worn-out coat
Flayed by the years: hoarse, almost voiceless memories cling
To paper time has turned yellow.
Weight of blood running down my back, toppling me.
How it hurts, seeing those pictures: I was running behind the
     eternal wheel,
Pounding it with my stumps, moving cycles along by instinct.

Dust falls, the fateful day falls, no appeal,
The day of general apocalypse when you sense
Your marrow begin to throw off sparks,
And a reverse torrent plunges upstream in your veins
A long time, long pain suffered drop by drop,
So much wine burning as the empty cup is raised.

Now they sleep behind adobe, sleep without answering.
They sink, face down, chewing stones,
And all the while their clocks fry in a dark pan.

How much pain is still left? From edges of old frayed masks
With nervous pupils, smoke rises and drifts
Across a face, a curtain of bone, and a tongue that long ago
Was already searching for you. In memory's chests a wind
Stirs through broken glass, adored skin, nails from another era.

So much lava: spit that cuts the table cloth of stone,
The infinite linen. Insult. I've been hung
On a spike of yours, harsh images follow me
And undulate on paper, there are screams, a breathing
Of birds above the current's scar.

Now talk to me,
Repeat in a still voice, here, into my deaf ear:
"Little bone of my womb, scorpion head, pearl of my eye."
If I'm sleeping, that's good: no need to be afraid. Mother,
Can't anything be done? Alright, then just give me a little while.
I'm coming. I'll bring you back these bones.

Funnel of Sand

Powerless to wake up, forced to remain in wounds
Like a smoking coal between my sheets,
Closing my eyes but there are no lids to cover the balls
That beat and glow red, and hearing in my pillow the sexual
Ghost of black darkness rising, skinless,
Without mouth or eyes to answer me, nothing, only a fevered
Hand made of thirsty nipples.

In my dream I turn over and beat on the stone mouth
Of a dry well, listening as a mare slowly climbs the steps
And sniffs at the silence that divides us: air
Dilates her nostrils more and more as she nears
The mill's mechanism, its ecstasy, the thousand-tentacled
Flow of the river in whose depths thirst swallows us.

Pulses along this thread keep tracing a body that is there
And not there, while dream licks its pistils. Its lips
Have never stopped crying, its long tongue tastes, curls,
Tightens the knots in my temples, eye-roots yearning to see.

Where is this woman, or her spirit? Mare of my rib,
Your multiple facets don't transform the light,
Don't open your skin's wall, your fur that rubs blind glass,
Alone, polishing a black ocean: your horizontal mane braided
With distant fallen feathers, with lives finished and sealed off.

I get up and listen. Where are those cries from? A blade
Falls, remorseless, and there's silence... Then slowly
Up a stairway in flames the desolated animal
Of my sleeplessness comes climbing. I only hear whispers
And footsteps, her trembling is in my ear, I pant
Under drills of rain and tear the past apart,
Leaving in my bed its scattered limbs, lust's favourite toys

That want to howl today, burning on the vine
Of her breath: I feel dry flowers blaze up under the fury
Of a new sun with claws, the most sensitive agent of pain.

Fanged snakes glide in scaled rings and on the bed her body
Unfolds, opened into halves: its thighs are wings
Crossing rivers in that storm-black gem, the night, and a rumour
Brushes my eardrum: her sex, butterfly whose flight
Is the opening of two lips at a feast of obsidian knives.

Broken Glass on My Pillow

The storm opens up. Tormented I listen to
A red-hot needle buzzing, foliage that changes colour
On my pillow drenched with blood, saliva, dream.
Then I run along a wall, endless stone,
Sealed-up balconies, rust, maybe nothing but a mask
That time withers and ravels into scraps.

My clothing wanders alone without my body, repeating gestures,
A magic game on a tightrope: it balances,
It descends like a slowly drowning man who penetrates the deep
Surrounded by bubbles, those great fish of his soul—the other I,
My brother, pulling an endless rope out of his mouth.

I grab this rope and tie it to the shore where metal
Flowers wilt, where his body is stretched out on the sand.
It seems to me that high overhead a monster is breaking into pieces.
Glass fragments fall, drift... The blades
Of a hurricane drag us... Wake up, wake up,
Someone shouts in my ear and under the clock, under its flint
I lash out in fear:
     Where—where are we?
       Condemned
To sink forever, to question those wounds over and over,
That body bristling with feathers and snow.
I feel blood running, beating in all my veins, cooling,
Asking once more for air, to burn, be flesh, be finally fire
That thrusts its tongues into night. Asking to sink
My head, nodding with sleep, into the wall and fasten my ghost
Who peers from mirrors, who drinks only from glasses full
Of vinegar: deep in the salt, the scar starts burning again.

Icicle

to Beatriz

You must have seen the demon goad, must have felt it
In your head when water turned to blades, when a voice hardened
And hung threatening in our window like a dart: each night
It grew, an immense being constructed of a thousand fixed pupils.
Water kept dripping cold and headlong down those nails,
A nightmare wind blew and needle-teeth gnashed.

One afternoon a pale sun obliquely touched the ice's skin,
The transparent body was dyed with blood and recalled its many
Lives: when it fell singing in waterfalls, when it was ocean,
Particle of clouds or pearls of sweat on a brow.
The ice spear was there twisting in the light
As if to inaudible music: other blades touched it
With their tips and made it bleed in the chest of ice.

I wonder who'll touch my spike, the thirst of the carrion
I drag every day through always darker emptier worlds.
Who'll blow as if by chance on my bones until
They sing what they've always known, that love is flame
And its caress changes ice into beating petals.

Of Petroglyphs and Photography

Leaning from the edge of a look-out, I examine the sketches
Someone etched into stone a thousand years back: a man-bird,
An iguana, a snake that stretches its skin
Across the rock like a river. Men standing
In a boat make signs and a harpoon plunges
Deep into the ceremonial night of a dream we're dreaming.
A being rises whose head is a huge pulsing sun
And it looks at us.
                  We look back. And under the grey sky
We exchange clothes with it. Beyond, the trees shut their circle,
The huge star of magic tenses new hides, and lightning strikes.

Now on photographic paper I see my son at the mesh fence
And I see that my open veins fit exactly over those designs.
Repeating the spells of fever traced there with a burning brand,
His mother lies back, asks a question, and changes into
The woman with a falcon mask on her shoulders. We are
Ghosts on the film that fixed us in greys on this paper.
Petroglyphs north of the present, an imprecise date:
I smile again for the photographer who returns in every age
And repeats the scene with other bones.

Only the sky changes. Sometimes it rains, sometimes blood falls.

The Marble Head

The marble head, the one born with me, the one that is coming,
Rolling from an eternity of cold iron, the one I can barely
Glimpse in the endless night of my ghosts,
When it weeps alone, more alive than I am in its fall.

The years turn slowly on their hinges.
I curl up on the ground, I wrinkle, I blind myself,
Powerless to understand why veins crack beneath the frost,
And a rictus honed on vertigo flees toward dream.

Its bones are the echoes of the perfect canticle, from temple
To temple crossing the faint blue lodes of a torrent
That bellows and welcomes time's weight on my pillow. Its eyeball
Burns among petals, blind as an iceberg drumming in the sea.

I ram that truncated head and jetsam worn by the tide
Rises like black waters, the hull creaks and grates,
My life unfolds on broken glass, my life the unknown number
And the thirsty knife-edges that mean blood.

Blood falls. Now rain is falling. Spiralling threads
Rise from acid to pass through the eyes of their needles.
Will we always be bound together, clay in pain, I
Crumbling stone and you the lightning, systole-diastole,
Skull of my other self rotting between the sheets,
Drowning, unable to return?

Let's wake up, my head, and break the red-hot iron with our brow.
Warm marble, sobbing delirium that falls and rises
From rancid bones, it smiles obliquely among thorns,
Its side splits, it shrouds itself in blood and begins to speak.

Ear-clock

My father took a clock apart and its two halves spread
Over the white tablecloth: multiple wheels like severed ears
Of a mechanical monster howling in secret as it crosses
Dials where the face of minutes and hours laughs.
Those diabolical parts were never pieced together again
And time ran freely there in my childhood.

                                                   Did years go by?
I don't remember. Again and again when making a poem, linking
Word to word, image to image, I've once more torn apart
The black numerals that imprison the man living inside me
And I've dragged the clock parts to the sea. The pieces float
And sink, nothing but ball bearings, wind-driven splinters,
Old papers that blow back to me and are a nothingness
Hollow to its utmost corners.

In the depths of a collage sometimes I hear my father laugh
Out loud, opaque millimetric time no longer exists and we can
Return to the kitchen table, hear my mother singing
Her melody of silence and see at the bottom of her pupils
The old miracle, the fleeting grace with which children look
At shining scissors as they cut up clocks on the sand.

Who'll set us free from our blind bell? From the horror-mechanism
In which I hear myself sobbing? Mystery, a wild mare,
Gallops out there in the dark. Hidden among branches
Of a pepper tree I hear birds warbling. Eternity passed by. Never
    waking,
My bones whitened by cold, I'm here, waiting for you.

The Bride and the Crow

Stretched out among branches, playing hide and seek with ghosts,
The bride huddles, her hair tangled with dead leaves.

She looks into the distance, never shutting her eyelids,
She grips her lover with her claws
While water changes colours in a fall and a thundering turbine,
Her desire, irises the black feathers of her bodice. But snow
Will protect her gown and the groom will peck at her eyes
With his compliments.

                    Your breasts are frozen pits, he says.
Poking and scraping, maybe I could mine you to the marrow
And make a nest in silence, near your heart, where the ticking,
The whirling, the mechanism's passion, a clock, grows still.

Your flesh is cool but Niagara's honey will never reach the sea.
If the wind opens your sex, other loving larvae, pins of ice,
Burrow inside you, the eye whistles over the storm,
Weariness undresses you and snow melts on your sides.

The guards will search for you with their dogs and find you by
        the rancid
Perfume of your thighs. They'll take you away, I know, and close
        up your eyes.
Good-bye, crow of my soul. My nerves are shreds. I've wasted
My days in loving you: our garden's lilies were plastic.

A Blaze with Feathers

Wings papyri catching fire in the sun
Wings folded and opened ever again in the game of hinges
Wings a river poured out in darkness
Wings whirling around a fruit armed with lightning
Wings burning in the feast of the repeated dream
Wings fastened to the transparent unique shoreless body
Wings whose feathers are warm turquoise
Wings thirsty for pleasure and like it fragile
Wings wasting away in the moon's bloodless knots
Wings migrating to other regions of the mind
Wings smiles wings over the snow of weariness
Wings all black covered with the ash of other wings that were
Wings broken by pain unable to advance
Wings symmetrical implacable wings of the clock of thirst
Wings tears in a waterfall that never ends
Wings with hard edges like a boiling crucible
Wings of cold slicing the nights of the knife
Wings syllables whirling around the word falling apart
Wings flying inward over the paper
Wings covering the body of forbidden pleasure
Wings as minute as the sweetness of that small insect
Wings of a fragile burning deity contained in sobs
Wings foam of another silent sea
Wings pity wearing away the torn images of those wings

Within the sun a warm memory of certain hands
Your nostalgia of a bird geometric projections of the wind

Encounter on the Rope

A man and a woman were walking from opposite extremes
Toward the point-zero where all threads meet.
They only knew each other by gestures and faces met in dreams,
Objects perfumed like wandering jewels,
Colours that switch off behind the glass.

Weeks went by, then months, and their shadows
Arched the cold sun of ice, high walls of crystal
Cried but the soundless cry never reached their lips
And they moved along their rope toward the edge of vertigo.

Now they were face to face, afraid to touch the impossible.
Their nerves tautened, she opened her eyes, he opened his mouth.
"I see a garden inside your forehead," he said. "I penetrate
Your mouth so desire will swallow me," she answered,
While their bodies disappeared.

                    Did anyone see ghosts
Can drink and eat themselves, skinless fruits of desires?

The White Pheasant

to Estela Lorca

All doors open on the night,
All birds fly toward the tree of tears and snow
Falls when you turn, it falls and seems to be the feathers
Of silence, that closed face of mist.

Now you open up, your eyelids part and your soul permits
Reality to those tatters of dream, the branches of lavender
That from one life to another carry the lines of a prayer
You alone know down time's feverish rivers.

All windows open on the torrent that boats mount
Through gorges on the moon-veins of a quartz mirror
Where the pity in your pupils glows for an instant
When you cry in the silence and the snow is warmer.

All faces open into a mask, always
The same grief-stricken image burning where pain
Echoes like a drum, the heart beats, begs for air:
Let me drink your tears, the perfume of mute sadness.

All's quiet here. Are we ghosts forgotten
In a grey house where no one calls? Is anyone listening?
Wind is erasing the snow's last traces. You must be
The white pheasant, and your eyes—aren't they
The ones that gaze at me in dreams?

Celluloid and Moving Images

to Karen Kane

In the first reel there were numbers that I can't
Remember. Tell me them. And then a whip on the scars
Of a man who hobbles along, bends over
And picks up a throbbing stone. Answer me.
The glass has to be broken, there's so much blood...

Light opens up, it closes. Maybe we're in a new
Scene: I see that a woman has bet on me, others laugh,
Mirrors splinter... I have no recollection of all this.
Only the wind comes back and talks about my childhood.

Second reel. "The dwarves also started small."
Dementia laughs and the truck grinds down
Its anguish-road. Innocent, the animals bleat,
Calling from a well with vermilion walls.

Light opens and closes. A river flows far off in the depths
Of your eyes. Who are you? What tears polished your bones?

Third reel. A man is walking in a glass box.
He doesn't find the person he was looking for.
He was looking for someone he does not find.
He leaves traces, cards, application forms no one understands.
A woman picks up his message and writes on it
With lipstick: Never here.

Does light open the trap-door above us and close it again?
Destiny, tick-tock, weaves its swift tapestry in iron.
It's snowing outside. Are you listening? My voice is guttural,
My English deformed. Won't you sew me into your side?

Exercises for the Third Hand

I

If I'm guilty beforehand, maybe I should understand
The padlock that bites the chain day after day.
It weighs on me like a curse to see you at the bottom of the mirror,
Orthopedic brother, condemned—they shave you without cause
And put gall you never asked for in your water.
Tell me, what hope do you have, why are you waiting?
                    No one will ever come back for you,
No one sings in the distance now, a knife scrapes over your face
And measures the bones of your forehead: your secret scar.
Beneath it, light closes her windows and seals her clocks.

II

I'm descending a staircase and I meet myself
Coming up, a stag's antler buried in my chest.
Please, some water, I say. I lie down in the last siftings
And question the wretched passerby; I insult my worm-eaten history,
Shouting and singing. And skinless now, I wrap my days in shells of
       wrath
And watch as they fall worn-out into a bottomless well:
Huge stones that suddenly go crazy and go out.

V

to Harald

On all fours I crawl along a knife-edge, turn back
And am a lizard, a quaternary animal; I cover myself in furs,
My scales creak: metal tears creasing each pane in the doorless
Hall of mirrors where someone is burning the days, root and branch.

The sparks are already going out on the anvil; cut down the middle,
My life opens and closes membranes on two faces of the world.
Pacing my room, an armadillo speaks, advising me,
But I can't remember what he says. I wake up. On the cold border
Where metal cuts its predicates, a hand quivers.
I don't see its destiny, its knotted lines, but only a freezing
Sandstorm and the relentless claw, and the howling.

VI

I see my father approaching down the road,
His arms outstretched. He is dead, I think, so how
Can he be here? He laughs at my doubts, sucking at the smoke
In his amber pipe. Figures rise out of it and the burning tobacco
Suspends lights above us like signs which, as they show themselves,
Polish the mirrors of the inner eye.

I laugh too. These are the landscapes I've dreamed,
The invisible city I wander through, hearing voices,
As I walk the desolate streets of an everyday labyrinth
Surrounded by desert.
                                    My father has to leave.
He hugs me. He takes a talking parakeet out of his chest.
He taps with his staff and the road opens up:
Now I hear, over my left shoulder, a mysterious
Transparent bird beginning to sing.

VII

to Hernán Baeza

I blow on the embers. Where are we? Outside the snow falls,
Tired eyes open over an infinite sea
Made of white pollen that deafens.
                                    Weeping itself
Is wrinkled and furrowed. Who's that calling out there? Who?
On the adobe wall hangs a *charrango*. Maybe it's he, my lizard
Grandfather, howling in pain, frost encrusting his skeleton.
And I am only a voice, a hide on which the tom-tom rhythm
Is beaten out, stretched over this clay that waited years for lightning
To strike it finally and forge it into a guitar.

VIII

to John Robert Colombo

When I wake up, I'm a Roman. Skeptical, I watch again
The stain that burns and covers the wall. What can I do?
One way or another the Empire is sinking
With all its screaming whores, and the barbarians,
Mallets in hand, are outside pounding,
Splintering the doors, pissing on the Carrara marble.
Will they ever learn that nothing matters? That nothing remains?
That everything was an illusion and that the heart beats for Rome?

The birds of my dream shriek far off; they leave the night behind,
They break against the sun or they awaken.

IX

On my crystal pillow I see the swift sheen
Of scales, a twisting rope that tightens around my neck as sour
As a sour fruit, and drags me, shredded, in the dust.

        I become aware of a crowd shouting,
They spit on me and lift me up on crossed poles,
I don't know why.

Then around my neck I feel not a rope
But a soft caressing hand that I remember: a flame,
The image of a young girl sitting in the forest. Her brother smiled
While David the Good sought to sketch the impossible.

The burning wood and smoking pitch bring before me,
On the tips of flames, these symbols in humming steel.
Now, I think, at last I understand Tibetan:
This is the beyond, here is my sentence,
The smoke of my rind in the wind.

X

I'm gambling and I watch hands shuffle
The cards, I hear a warm panting, but it's very dark
And I can't see the face of the one who in dreams
Bets against every signal on my road.
I lose the days, I lose the baggage of my past. Maybe
I lose my bones, I lose the blood in which I could have written
The Name, but in the flames I win a pupil
That lets me see someone who is running in the depths,
Who goes up in smoke, flees in the shadows, becomes nothing...

What difference does it make now?
Who was he, after all, who hid his face from me for so many years?
In the dark eyelid of the night I hear him crying.
And sometimes I wish that I could hear his broken panting again,
Listen once more to his breathing that goes past, comes back,
And bursts apart, ripping to shreds the cards that are my life.

XII

Alchemical Wardrobe
a painting by Susana Wald, 1984

A man inside an amber box believes he is living a dream
When he opens up his belovèd. He doesn't clearly understand
What is happening, why the wall turns on the sea's hinges
And his panting, like a moving train, crosses the eyes
Of night. High above them, a woman envies the couple and doesn't
     see
The cause of this burning waterfall, stones from the heavens.
A delirious aroma of mandrakes harries and shepherds the moon into
The mirrors. The beautiful one takes up a branch green with leaves.

XIII

on a sculpture by David Pelletier
Art Gallery of Hamilton, Ontario

Yesterday I saw the ventriloquist. In the posture of ancient Egyptians
The man and his doll sat in a white, polished truth
Like a father who notices in his son's eyebrows
The long forgotten traits of his grandfather.
                    And it hurts me to see these two.
It was as though my femur suddenly flowered into words,
And I heard my father sitting on my knee, repeating the same
Anguished questions, beyond the frost, about the ghost of dust
That takes us away... But looking into their eyes I saw no tears:
They kept questioning each other, inventing answers, submerged
In each other like parts of a whole—the water flowed down a single
        mirror.

I don't know if, when I write, an echo sounds on a distant drum:
The same letter, the same name. Or if in speaking I only repeat enigmas
In a dream. I roll on my bed and maybe someone else is asking my
        questions
Down there in the pit: maybe strings are lowered and shaken in darkness
And I'm the dummy and the ventriloquist, the one I saw yesterday,
And today he's crying.

XIV

A woman was dancing, and on the rope my double and I, naked,
Spinning rapidly, followed her despite the lances of the leather
Clock. Is the lava finally burning? Does the pollen swing
Its lamps, the gold of light, above those bodies?
Little more than a dream, something like a melody, her fingertips
Engraved her name repeatedly on the current. Days go by.
Weeks grind across the window. If she came back,
If she finally returned, maybe the rain
Would wash this blood off of us.

          My breastbone hurts me. My time hurts me.
Don't cry anymore. Things aren't so bad. Let's drink those tears:
Pass me the glass of salty sweetness. Let's gather our bones back
     together.
And you can tell me: does that doll you're hiding talk to you
     in dreams?

XVII

If I was once a splinter hurting you,
Sand between your lips or simply a castaway
Who in his anguish signals with burning leaves,
The light of an unreadable hieroglyph, on the white sand
Beaches of your body…

The heaving sea: that eternal lust, the green
Layers that cover you—once, then a thousand times
Passing across your eye and veiling it—a nacreous sap
That takes the form of crying, the sinuous form of tears...

The sea, all lace: its spindrifts are your legs,
Scissors that bite at vertigo with their crux.
A cup of sweetness, you offer yourself in a ceremony
Of roots that cut the deep-hidden sun into blades.

XVIII

to Alejo

Two scorpions in a bottle ask why
Such crystals exist. Near them two lovers roll
Furiously on the grass, trying to hook bone
To bone, soften their edges, polish their lips
And go beyond the burning skin, that lens
That lets the unattainable be seen.

                    Desire sheds its leaves
And the couple, emerging from the dream, tosses a stone
And breaks the bottle, setting the scorpions free.
Perhaps none of the four knows that waves are trapped
In the green crystal and deep in that ocean spores burst:
There the foam of ecstasis, its currents, climb the night again.
And in the cell of sparkling glass, phantoms have devoured
Each other for a million years, swarming from the egg. They laugh,
Pulling on ropes, pulling downward into the depths, where torrents
Howl out, in a thousand scales, the fate of the days: the deadbolts.

XXI

Concierto

a painting by Cosme Tura (1430-1495)

The three are singing on a balcony. It is as though time
Had stilled its antennae and each of them could hear the song
That celebrates eternal spring. The lute player in the centre
Strums his instrument, marks the tone and gazes at an abstract
Point where lyrics and emotion join. The beautiful Bianca
Caresses his right shoulder; her whole being in her voice rises to fly
And be the essence of the words, poetry. No doubt that Cosme knew
When drawing her the warmth of white marble, a breath, a grace
Moving within things. A young man sings behind them, lifts his voice
And rests his hand on the railing. Whoever has heard this song knows
That time burns like the Rose of Sharon. Yet the three are there
And sometimes I feel the threads of their voices: they insist, in the
    square cell
Inlaid with sparks, that love is eternity and in singing it they know.

XXII

to Mario Cesariny

Sitting on the edge of my bed, paralyzed as before an abyss,
I contemplate the jaws of the new day, those rigid iron bars.
What can I do? I see my foot growing into five toes,
Prolonging itself into nails, into iron shoes and pedals.

My other foot is still in my dream, the locomotive of night
That weeping tides drag till it crashes against the limit.
Suddenly the sheets seem to me an immense mollusk
Full of soft ardor, drifting in some impossible time.

But now a two-faced moon arraigns my image in its depths,
And I smile to see my double repeat my gestures. To watch his face
Hurts me: his eyes so wide, so pained. I, who half split open
The segments of hell, can see him rowing down his wounds.

XXIII

The clapper shrills, and the black bell of the telephone
Wakes me on the heights of dawn. Who's there?
I hear a sound of brakes, and a shattering of mirrors that repeats
My question but from the other side, from beyond bitter
Mirror-silver depths: Who's there? Someone is calling
As if from inside a tunnel, our numbers are joined, they copulate
And become black shreds in the filthy nest of the telephones.

XXV

The woman on the trapeze: lust in my childhood eyes
Watching the crested bird fly from one mast to another
In the huge tent. That apparition in her shining mail
Comes down from her height, the green costume shines like scales.
Where could she be today? The wind whirls the images

Across the bottom of my skull. More than woman, she would glide
Along the wire in melodious flames like a drop of sweetness.
The silk of her skin barely contained her.

                         Today, turning my eyes
To the past, I sometimes find mysterious threads that repeat the game:
A woman laughs like a hinge, the wind breaks lamps,
It flurries the wings of someone who wants to fly, be feathers,
Be, in the net that memory wove, a chimera soaring.

XXVII

But what species are we, our soul shrouded in wolfskin?
A tin can for a hat, all of us rolling down the stairs
Till we reach the sea, where ice breaks the windows.
Our steps have died out. If only I could wake up.

Then I go back down the dark ramp that sinks
To the bottom like a conch shell. Eyes watch me from my plate.
With my knife I scrape the hard surface, the cornea of my days,
I bring fragments back together, fallen hairs that I find
In the suitcases barking next to my bed, bored with waiting.

The porcelain is moaning. Flexing the rubber of his perfect shroud,
An armadillo speaks to me of the past. I break him in two. He laughs.
I get my bones ready for the trip, my breast devoured
By a billion insects. There exists an everyday darkness,
And in my ears a drum sounds. It's late already.
It's always, forever, late.

Listening to Venus

Snow covered my life and that white ash mixed broken mirrors
With mud, remains of furniture with childhood love,
Faces extinguished by the days' remorseless passing,
Dreams that surface and sing in a dark alembic
Where I talk and argue with beings now dead, waiting
For the soft, precious emerald of light to visit me at last:
I came into this world to dream it, not be the metal that they hammer.

Because I know: She is coming along the motionless river of
    frankincense
And myrrh, invisible perhaps to us, blind
Beggars who wait for her, wakeful, nailed to the astrakhan
Doors of night, listening to her howling laughter,
To echoes of her voice, the only water that could give us peace.

Preferring a Dream

Waking and seeing her at the foot of the bed,
Ready to leave, her hair gathered in a knot,
He hesitated for an instant, but then said:
I love you more now than during the night
When fever and desire imprison you in petals.

Offering him her mouth, she repeated: See you soon!
And he pressed his eyelids to avoid watching her leave.
He knew that in the dream, a moment before, she,
Completely naked, had smiled at him in a street that doesn't exist;
And maybe she'd return in another dream, to time eternal
Where lilies moan under the passing steps of the wind.

The Eyewitness

I went into the studio and you were there naked,
Opened into two sections like a hinge.
Yet it was sweet to see you and watch you as the sun
Wandered on the walls and its light dreamed you.

Then in the depths of the canvas I saw an eye
That looked into mine, and it was as though the Other
Were burning my marrow. I turned back again to see your image
And you were a shadow. The barbed sun polishes its flints.

Leaving, I thought of the one who painted that eye
There on the canvas, light at the end of a tunnel;
Maybe we're only an instrument
That revolves on itself, and our body, a butterfly
Of warmth, fluttering, crosses the moon in mirrors
Of pleasure and dream. The canvas is still there, an image
Repeated from another image, and you and I come apart:
Eyewitness of the knot of waters flowing away.

Anniversary Stone

homage to René Magritte

At the window: the eye, a blue stone,
The stone in love with the Sargasso Sea,
The stone clenched in the hand like lichen
Or like a seashell that dissolves itself in its own tide.

The stone in a room where no one ever comes,
Fixed on the rug like someone talking to himself,
Axe that is only an eyelid, or a lip brushing the scar
That is day, each day: mark where the sea tore, opening its hinge.

The beating stone, as warm as the horrifying skin
That covers the knot now screaming in the forest.
The stone that fell from the black hole
Behind the sun, the one that is coming,
Turned to coal by a billion years or degrees of love.

The soft, worm-eaten nightmare stone
Of seeing the grinding moon with just one eye,
And waiting for someone, a gentleman in a hat,
A bound breast, a sex on fire, to come,
Sink his teeth into the apple, and burn this silence.

Coffee with Blood

Today I saw a child gazing at his misfortune. His tears
Have dried away, in his misery he has only one eye left:
He has no palms, they took the hands that might have covered
His grieving face, their gaff smashed the window, they burned his clock.

I've seen his desolate gesture and would rather be someone else.
It makes me ashamed to have hands and not be innocent,
To have my fingers and move them, to use my eyes and never see
Bitter injustice like a plain hard thing, bitter and senseless.

What can I give this child, if a tear can never again
Flow back to its sea? I would like, above all things,
To be God and give him back what they took, what belonged to him,
His eyes and his hands: his innocence.
                                And give him forgetting,
So he can see at last that destiny is the arabesque
A bird draws at the will of the wind, the cyclone's wing.
Maybe he could smile again.

Today I saw this child and I don't understand why;
How misfortune can ever strike this way,
This deep, and pour so many miseries into a steel cup,
Stirring them to red heat, without sugar: coffee and blood.

A Maker of Infernos

to Martín Cerda

Religion class, room three; there Father Gregorio
Will explain to us, forty rascals, the mechanisms
Of eternity:
        "Consider (he says) the passing of time in hell:
Once every century a blue ant completes one trip
Around a bronze sphere as big as the Earth. Slowly,
Step by step, it wears away that gleaming metal star.
Ten thousand myriads of footsteps fall, repeating themselves,
And when it's done...only one second has passed
In God's inferno of torments."
           He'd stop there, and we:
Chattering with stupor and fright, we'd beat our heads against
    the windows.

Don Gregorio Martínez, Jesuit professor of rhetoric,
Is dead: the worms, as though they were ants, drag him away.
Thank heaven that each of us rascals is now free
To choose his own inferno.

Ethiopian Woman with Inlays of Abalone

Butterflies, incarnate sweetness, strike the neon tubes:
Fluttering for centuries, selling their flesh, the foam of all the races,
Offering themselves to fire, surviving like fallen timber
That burns as it drifts, they open their multicoloured bodies,
They hear the song of those who tattooed their far-off childhood.

Five liters of blood mixed with water, the captives
Warble like doves; offering their antennae to pleasure,
They enter and leave the furnace.
                              What word game, what syllables
Etched on ivory could exist between us? You question a mirror,
But wind has scraped away the silver from the back of the sun,
And music on your lips is only nostalgia for another thirst.

Night, stretched over the sands, on your now glowing body
Plays the sorcery of abalone, the magic shells
Of a perfect braided spiral, from sex to head, the scales,
The feathers of a vertiginous Being, unseen inside you
Whirling its forbidden threads.

Remembering in the Wax

to my mother

My mother gave me a candle the colour of birds
So I could light it and hear the wick of her laughter;
Months passed, became years, and now
As I watch that quivering struggling flame
I feel the wax fall and hear only silence in its petals.

What did those tears that misted the mirrors
Mean to tell me? Tired now, my mother goes on dragging
Her feet through ashes; the light of the hives has been put out,
The concrete is shattered, the doors bricked up forever.

Only memory multiplies her image. Sometimes I hear voices,
She seems to wander through the house again
But there's no shadow here, only a beating of wings, a flock
Crossing the night as it drifts south.

A knife whittles her silence into shavings, the dark
Crushes her shoulders, a rain has started to fall.

The Lovers' Descent

We turned off the lights and lay down on the floor,
Like insects that crawl along the veins of a log
Of driftwood dragged by storms, and colliding with each other
We went down slowly into the maelstrom's tearless eye.
Once the walls of our prison were broken open,
We loved one another without solace,
Offering words in an unknown tongue, each conjuring up
The other's ice, that eternal ticking in the chest.

Asleep—are you asleep now? On the shores of an unknown
Ocean, your flayed thighs are fishes like birds,
Whitened by foam, remnants waiting for another light,
Where their broken wings can burn to death again.

The Invisible Presence

to Frida and Laurens Vancrevel

To open the days like opening our eyelids,
Drop all the dead weight at last, leave (carefully
Turning on the lights), pass through walls as though they were
Doors, a vertical sea that closes into lips.

Without feathers, and now without hooks to sink into the flesh,
Skeleton of today, to slip away invisibly like someone parting
    the wind,
And whisper into the sleeper's ear the syllables
That could wake him—blue gramophone of memories.

To watch as the beautiful one rises out of torpor, eternal,
Unreachable, and gestures, smiling at herself in the mirror.
To have power to move petals through the storm that is her head,
To pluck the strings when she asks herself the why of silence.

To float on waters, spin in the whirlwinds, be dust
In the desert where the strange caravan comes closer,
Bringing me the key, a warm nostalgia in each hieroglyph
When snow falls between hands and makes them translucent.

Once more to find the centre of the cruel labyrinth with no walls,
Knowing that someday, in front of the mirror where fleeting
Surfaces burn, we will be just a name. To love only the essential,
The scent of leaves, the belovèd one, invisible presence.

If the Comet Returns

to Susana, who was waiting for the comet too

When the comet returns—if it does return—
Everything will be different and we won't be able to follow its flight
In the stained lenses. You and I under the earth,
Indifferent, will sleep one inside the other, with our bones
Braided into the dust, bleached by lime and forgetting.

Blood won't run in our veins and remnants of our skin
Will flutter, frayed threads in the wind. We might be
Ash that someone clenches in his hands,
Then throws into the torrent, thirst's pelt of thorns.

When the comet returns, you and I, like the stars, will plough
The sky in a wandering bubble where desire and love are living coals.
In the eternal stream, maybe nothing but a tear.

Erase the Traces

It was useless: the truth was impossible to convey.
—Álvaro Mutis

He spoke of leaving but never revealed the way.
He moved lights in the wind. His trunks full of stones
Glowing red-hot, shapes caressed by his fingertips, imaginary
Sails for the flight, the hurricane's skin seduced him.

The night fogs of harbours devoured him, worn out.
Torches began to move, and compasses shattered,
Their needles burned in the unknown, in that very hour
When, opening the lips in silence, one touches bone.

He kept descending in a spiral, pupils whitened by a vision
That could only be the ocean boiling in eddies. He left
No letters, his fever-drawings were erased, they burned his wall.
If he ever wakes up, he'll see blood: this world is the Other.

Image of Doubt

to Olga Orozco in her labyrinth

Rain falls on plains of kaolin and, as always, men
Are moving across them, weak beings at the beck
Of any wind. Fire erects its crest, lava glints,
And this Sacred Face of the Mothers elaborates itself.

First-and-last syllable of our language, invisible
When life spins the diamond, flashing its facets,
Stretching skin over the faces that multiply,
Elongate, touch borders of burning mercury,
A dizzying window on the waters.
                                        A pilgrim trudges
With his pack of horrors slung over his back,
Leaning on a stick, leaving some traces
In the wet ash. And behind him the woman, small and fragile,
With a child hanging at her side, follows in those prints
Among blue-crested birds and elephants as slow as rivers.

                        And then she turns to one side
And looks at an acacia with whistling thorns.
"She wants to see beyond and, like all of us,
She feels a moment of doubt and then continues her march
Northward."
                        A million years ago, a myriad
Of seasons with their days, nights and deaths, someone
Looked back and for one second was allowed
To hear the river of faces screaming, beaten into dust
On a merciless anvil, where blood flows under the weight
Of memory when it smiles in dreams and tears fall.

Coming to the End of the Blind Knot

to Gwendolyn MacEwen

Tired of living, your sail shredded by your ruined nails,
Your body—frost garrotes it, it huddles in fear,
It harries the crows, and on a blank horizon blood
Freezes. Can't you hear anymore, don't you feel pain?
Maybe you've deciphered the monstrous, mysterious hieroglyph
That burns between our lips and never forgives, the Word
On the anvil? Closed over yourself, you drift downstream
With no sorrows, memories or scents to paint your eyes:
A fiery needle sewed them shut forever and now you've become
Only an image, a cipher at the end of the blind knot.

Woman Under the Lindens

Are you pure accord, both instrument and woman,
A flower burning in the invisible? Blindly
We look at you, and tattoo you whom we cannot see,
Creating signs to recall you, a mirage to be your skin.
You come to us trembling as if a mystery had touched you.

I drowned myself in you and at the bottom of your eyes
Half saw the dream we never can decipher:
Across your face floats a swarm of petals,
Music of the desire to be: to be with you,
To be the sun in the blood.

There, in a perfectly held trilling, I burned
On pulsing snow: your skin. The boundaries between words
Erased themselves and, from within, a graceful air
Burnished you. Tears were warm, moons were gliding down
To nest on your shoulders.
                              Are you still there?
The days keep passing, I hear only echoes,
Crumbs of a ruined forgiveness, and the coming cold.

The scar of desiring you starts to hurt again.

Body of Insomnia

Your image is incised on the inside of my eyelids,
So time for me is dream, a shroud, a torturing
Flame, and—when I hear the hurricane air
Inflate my chest—the thirsty ghost that drinks you.

A grey mist falls, under my sheets a tide roars out
And I want to crush you to me until I feel your marrow—
So close and far away—and I want to bury your head
Near my heart, near where that drum of dust lies beating.

Because it hurts to know that you are here somewhere dreaming
With open eyes, that day after day you rise up like a bird,
Gossip with the sun, paint your eyes with ultramarine kohl,
And you don't know why you cry and wait, or if you are the miracle.

The night is long and insomnia drags out memories
That whirl downstream while you, my dove, my bird-moon,
Circle desire, its coruscating gems, your body
Covered with petals, foam of an eternal tide.

Will I always have to be blind to see you? Always
Have to wait for a miracle? Each day the millstones
Of this destiny grind away. And the burning lines that harrow
Your hands and mine. And this mouth—this wound.

Sketches of Insanity

Galloping toward the sea, crossing the sands at last
To open the doors, biting my lips down to the frost.
Descending the spider's stairs to hang from a thread
And blow the gleaming conch covered with spines.

Sailing upstream along your forehead of a white-shining Amazon
Who questions in her vigils the end of the wind in the sails.
If you could, you would burn up all feathers with a breath.
Bent, your shoulders are warm cataracts, and the quartz beats.

Turn your ear-trumpet, your clock of curare, toward me. Your story
Will always be the same, since you always sharpen your loved one
Till you strike bone. Let's draw the splinter out of the dove,
Turn the days back, lay you on the drumhead and bleed you.

You break needles, clock hands, spires, put a dromedary in a bottle,
Hide a jewel that rears up at the tightening of your thighs.
You admit you are a siren but conceal your flame-stroked tail.
In the depths of your eyes green riders go coursing by.

Look at your palm. Can you hear? Just an echo of crying,
Rain's dizzying freshness as it falls. You empty yourself out,
Become an urn: you want to drink all things blue, all blueness,
Bit by bit, you repeat the intricate weave of a forgotten tongue.

Lover and Cannibal

A friend was saying: to cannibals alone
Is it given to enjoy the heart's flavour,
And we all laughed, thinking of green
Grasslands and lianas through which each one of us
Goes tracking the prey that he or she has picked,
Surrounding it with sparks, riddling it with darts
Until it's trapped immobile in a net of loud voices
And whispers, wrong numbers ringing on telephones,
Doors slammed shut through which an eye
Had pierced to the opener's marrow and gone silent...

Today there's no sacrifice to any goddess, no one
Sees the direction of our march, when someone falls
Between points or edges it's solely by accident,
Blood spreads over the street amid loud cries.
Who fired the dart? Who gathered the slivers of glass
On the altar cloth, preparing the ancient ceremony?

Today I see myself sleepwalking: I drink you
Little by little, open your lips with a hot coal, throw myself
Down into you as though fallen from a cliff—defying hazard,
Plunging through your veins till I touch the knot, the pulsing
Drum that beats in you.
                                The tom-tom deafens me,
My eardrums are destroyed but now I can bite,
Possess, grapple myself to the mollusk I adore in you,
That bitter tint with its taste of salt and blood
In which last remnants of the ancient songs are burning.

The days devour me and I devour your image,
Which is holy. A sound of rivers falling, of the storm
Bellowing, pierces my temples. We go on and on
Across the ice, light-blinded, and thirst's torment
Attenuates our bones till they shatter to bits in the cold
And blow away.

I smell your body's perfume,
Resin of amber that the cannibals burned
Ages ago: Listen. Can you hear?
                              Each and all discovering
The salt taste within them, offering themselves as Gift,
Giving themselves in love and piercing, descending, falling
To the deepest stratum of dream.

On the Kama Sutra

If a woman opens the sun, comes down
The azure stair of her desires, enters a garden
And is in herself the mirror of a thousand faces, a whirling
Seed that is multiplied, burns brilliantly and goes out,
A cloud of fragrance scattered by the wind.

If she is seen only in profile, her thighs and her arms
Driving forward while her hair falls quiet
Like a curved helmet over her neck, and perhaps unknowingly
Her body repeats an inward image, because real things are only
Reflections of what the river drags here from time's source.

When she turns her back to the one watching her,
Undresses, is naked in the water, with only jewelry
Of liquid pearl to cover her, and looks left and right
Holding her breath, and her body, consumed by a light breeze,
Becomes those flowers in flame that burn on the river.

When all images are reunited in the central knot
Of her labyrinth (the sun no longer throws shadows on the bodies,
All the heat-enervated legs and shoulders, in the marble asleep),
Her breasts, erect for pleasure, become transparent
And turn into what I dreamed: two doves in flight.

Only her lips' freshness, the cool foam of her smile
Clothe the curve of the sacred womb with their torrents,
And flow on until they reach her wild orchid sex.
Slim hands for her light touches: she alone knows how
To say the sweetness of the saffron milled in her bodies.

Servant who carries her perfume: is this my fate? Azure
Water dimples under the wind's step. A snake hisses, looped
In the restless almond tree of desires, and freighted with petals
The river runs to its sea: pleasure undiscovered and denied.
Open: you are love's lip, its eye without limits. Open.

The Tired Mirror

I am no longer waiting for another day, another woman
To discover herself before the immobile river of my being,
And smile as she examines the tracks that time is leaving
In her skin, rich loam today, a second later hard and wrinkled.

They came a thousand years ago, and never change, yet every one
Who draws near to herself on the balcony of my reflections
Is new. They look at themselves not seeing the eyes that watch them
In the depths of this glass, this hearse, this hurricane of silver.

But the years turn and from one life to the next I hear
The same song repeat itself, I see the same faces
Grimace as they re-touch that mask, taking up again
The gestures of the pride, the secret passion, that devours them.

My days have no direction but waiting for rain, a rain of lye
That might finally husk the painful scales of silver
From my body. Blind, I keep falling, broken into pieces
By the cries and shouts that rise out of dark Lethe's tide.

The Taste of Salt There Is in Rain

Today it rained all wrong and then on the snowdrifts
The rain became glass. It was a drumbeat
Of deaf hammers across that hide of vast distances:
They fell in a torrent, they opened into a riverbed,
A sea that was searching for the sea, a grey cataract.

From on high today a response rolled down,
The falcon wheeled, carrying his talons past at eye level,
The green of the pine forests became more green.
The deaf noise vanished, a lone dove that crosses
A far sky, the grieving of one who remembers the Ark.

Water drips and in blind days I hear
Time trickling into phials and cascading
Into the pit: eyelids don't open in this solitude
That harries me, soaked to the bones,
Water hammering on water.

Where are the sun, the feathers, coolness?
                                        The rain has
A hidden pain, a salt taste of the one who waits for you
In your dreams and probes your skin when you come, listening
To what is inside you, as the sun hisses and cracks.

Desperate Man

for A. F. Moritz

Albrecht Dürer found it there under acid as he scraped off
The wax that covered the years: those fissures, the grimace
That appears suddenly, a blind gracelessness making the machines
Run backwards. Could it have been death throwing its dice?

Or a knotted flux of tears striking the root? Fifty years
Turn anyone who cries into a scar harrowed in dust.
The needle ran down his back of embellished copper
Leaving its trace there:

                              A man, lying on the ground,
Desperate, struggles to keep skull and mandible pressed shut,
So the thunderous scream that silences birds in flight
Will not escape from his chest, tumescent with pain.

The others—mere faces, round bodies humbled by plague—
Are only phantoms on the shores of an abyss
That opens forever each time, Albrecht, you separate paper
From inked metal incised by sorrow and bitterness.

And there we are, where it hurts to be: on the edge
Of an open wound. Ashes are burning in our sides.

An Experience with Surfaces

I cut a strip of paper, twisted it, and glued the ends.
On this I wrote your name with images in your likeness.
I began cutting that wheel lengthwise and got two rings,
Their edges interlaced. Where was the inside? Where
Was the outside? Thus on the Möbius strip your image,
Your name, was multiplied, repeated on the white
Paper, dissolved into letters, into tremulous sounds
Murmuring prayers in a language I didn't recognize.

You remind me of a strange perfume. Is that everything?

Emergency Number

From the far side of the garden I listen to the storm
Bellowing, bee-swarming, weaving a wall from words.
I listen in emptiness to an unheard sentence, threats
That a knife will cut the strings of the lute forever.

I get up from desperate straw and recite by heart
The exact numbers of her name. I repeat them in reverse.
Where are we?
                I hear a far-off burning
Of skeletons now free from painful flesh. Sirens are crying
And insanity, drunk on sleep and dream, sings in my ear.

On a Photograph of Ezra Pound

in memory of Larry Wallrich

Here is his face, here are its eyes, embers
Burning in a sea of wrinkles, the poet
Inscribed by life.
                    At last his ship has reached Venice.
He is not Ulysses and no Penelope awaits him,
The stones are deafened by injustice and mocking voices,
This shadow of music on the water.

Who will chant the trobar now that night is coming down?
Fragile is the marble and emptied of its classic grace;
The old man watches the sea, the solitary jetty where long ago
Beauty tempted him, a sudden bright blare from the sirens' horn.

But did this ever happen? Tiger in a filthy cage
For days and nights devoured by thirst, vexed by brutal
Neon light. Traitor to what?
                            Reptilian Usura crawling,
Giving to the plastic flower its synthetic scent.
Disease. Slag. Scrap...
                        Far away there in Pisa. Who remembers?

Injustice is bitter and marks those it touches forever.
Maybe his error was to discover harmony and break
Hatreds over his own shoulders, because it hurts
To see we are only this: a man walking, yet rooted
Fast in the cauldron of madness where Confucius and Cavalcanti
And Duccio de Buoninsegna are illegible letters on a shadowed slate.

Where is the sea you loved? Haughty agèd Ezra,
Again let your ears gather the warm iridescent questions
Of the sun, half open your eroded palm where the lines burn
Like the damned in torment.
                              We have come to the end
Of all roads, and there are no questions, no sphinxes.
What are poets for?
                    Here is the hurricane.

Carrying Rocks on Her Back

on a painting by Betty Spackman

A woman drags her decaying flesh, she paints it with grease,
Rubs it with her hair and over months brings out its luster.
She wants to reach the earthenware jar of water singing far off,
But again and again Jesus, who is her lord, cuts his hands
And in a bowl mixes earth with blood.

On the hard clock the knife of years divides us
And this woman returns by the same road; her glow
Has gone out and the ball of her eye, lidless, is crying;
The panniers' inhuman weight is breaking her back.

Standing stooped in a pond, she tries to grasp the bandages,
The worn-out leather thongs, that bind her life.
Day after day thorns hurt her, the sharp glass edges
In her images: sarcasm, violent, like spit.

And she looks at his face, the eternal Face
That must have a soul behind its decaying flesh.
She contemplates his stumps and no tears come. Today
The other hand, the one that grows within, tightens her painless
Harness straps. Who wears those nailed hands for us?

The Warning

Reviewing days and years now gone like scattered
Cards of a November's end, I asked myself:
Will I have ten more years to let my life race,
Decipher love, find the Word?

Then suddenly they called. I had to go. I covered myself
In winter hides. Ahead of me my wife and son were walking.
There was our truck, sunk in its yellow paint.
It had to be moved and we pushed it with all our might:
As if sand tried to open the sea.
Then a man came to help us. Thanks. We pushed again
And slowly the wheels began to turn.

It was then that I saw her: she was gesturing to me
From the end of a tunnel, her face covered with a black veil.
A brutal wind, razor that unleafs the trees, was blowing.
Where can the birds be now? She smiled and walked away.

Next morning I heard a bell burning. One after another
They tried to reach me, a swarm of telephone voices.
My daughter came to visit, we were in a strange house. Was she
    still asleep,
Was she better now? I listened to her climb the stairs. I'm here, I
    shouted,
In the invisible spot in the kitchen. She didn't hear.
A face on the wall studied me: it was the veiled skull
That sees itself in my eyes.
                 I was waking up.

I didn't question the transitory burning of those images.
I heard the birds sing again. For them time doesn't exist.
They live eternity, they are song alone.

(Night of 29-30 November 1989, Toronto)

126

Doubled Up on a Table I Listen

Doubled up on a table I listen to pulleys lift
And lower. Years lost deaf and dry on this dust. At night
Sometimes I talk through the cell's wall of salt
To the me there on the other side and start to sob.

Why this anguish, this star that reels
Burned to an ash in yesterday's sky? I lean back
On the plank hard as a board for laying out a corpse.
No answers. If only I could tie the knot of words
That would be a channel for this howl, this memory
Of blind creatures I can't manage to forget.

But at last I feel my body stretched out in a river
Of warm marble that smiles, rocks me, and puts its question
In the cracks of the ceiling, its nails, its why.
                                        Never again will my table be
Just a table, now that I see beneath tense young skin
The blood running away. Do you hear me? Traveling these limits
Is meeting God, reaching the edge of the desert
That rears the winds. The rain has begun.

Laughing, I Told My Dream

to Susana Wald
for her painting on the same theme

Laughing, I told my dream: a huge bird carried me
Back to my childhood desert. It was dark and the Bird
Was descending to the salt flats in the Valley of the Moon.
Everything glowed from within and in front of us,
Boiling like the lines in my palm, stood a wall,
The prodigious wall that reaches to the sky.

A woman, staring into my eyes, approached and said,
I've been waiting centuries for you; go back to the beginning
Of beginnings, penetrate into this wall where Life is trapped
And gestated.
            I felt a tom-tom thrum in my ears,
I advanced against the wall, skin of mist, sweetness
Of the deepest dream, the one that carries us
To her, the Many, the Adored, she whom the wind kisses.

I've never come back. I don't know why I'm at this table
Covered so deep in feathers, names, and petals,
Laughing with you, answering your questions absently.
Understand that, as I tell you my dream, I am still there.

"La cola es al collage..."

to the poet Juan Jorge Bautista

I've cut up all the papers. I've arrived
At that border of age from which one looks back on the disaster.
Everything is spilled on the ground, knives and colours and papers,
Waiting for me to return with a knot of fever from my pillow
And permanently glue a bird's foot to the moon,
A sun to an eye, a green to a yellow.

Dust falls. Scratching and scratching, I find the beatific
Señoras, their hats and stockings, their underthings of leather.
What goddamned garbage!
        All those ladies moth-eaten in their tombs,
Seeds of another sun: the engraver gave them one more century
And I see them passing through their pages
In an old book, other Beings, almost the same butterflies as once.
The scissors don't judge. They cut out inked scraps and the scorpion
    those women
Kept hidden between their thighs leaps out.
Now they don't remember,
They're only half-machine half-female things. They show their hearts
Through the plumes of a fan time flutters.

The Second Deluge

It was raining pitchersful and the black clouds were stuck
Above the old house. Not knowing it wasn't a ship,
They beat on its time-crumbled bricks.
                              Like threatened birds,
My children ran from window to window watching the water
Cover the lawn.
                    Beatriz came and asked in a small voice,
Ludwig, tell us, you know—is this the Flood?

Nothing for me to do but prove the opposite: we took
Our clothes off and ran out together in a gang
To dance happily in the downpour.

                              Now I don't know,
I speculate. The holy books say that when the day comes
The sky will open into metal birds.
                              Will we hear
The thunder? The flashing of the blind light?
The second Flood will be fire and we'll be pebbles
The hurricane takes from this world to the next—just dust.

Today I Came Across the Machete of Wrath

Today I came across the machete of wrath, the one the Chinese
Use for splitting a lacquered swine stretched over a log,
And quicklime boiled into spume, dogs burst from their pounds;
I'll love you naked on that beam, with a single blow I'll sever
Your twenty digits, your forty nails reeking with honey,
And I'll begin my work:
                        The legs must be spread wide open
So the accumulated frost of years can be scrutinized
In the depths of your lips. The lover-edge will keep slicing you
Apart. Go on, plead in vain. I'll wait to hear phosphorus
Flowing down your back, that ancient papyrus of insult.

I'll wipe the rain from my brow so I can see inside you
And tear your magic breasts into sections, the breasts that give
Acid oil for the hoisting of so many pulleys. You won't be
Able to tell us then that two minutes of light are enough.
I'll cut up your holy scriptures that are rust and brain-shard
With bitter gusto, no lemon needed when fried in blood.

Today I came across the machete of wrath and on second thought
Decided not to buy it. I'm revolted by showy display,
This fetish of ripping the scales from the cruel siren is nothing
But to taste other acids, happen upon other routes,
Keep on breaking mirrors that give back the image of a ghost.

For a Savage Love Mounted Bareback

I'm dying of love and you don't understand...
I hissed between my teeth. She turned to me then
And looking deep in my eyes harshly she asked me:
Can you keep upright on a mare? Dive into fire
Till your eyes burst and the sun burns down?
                              I stayed quiet; slowly
I tightened the reins on the hitching-post. When she finally
Quit talking I opened her hide from the neck to the lips
She carries hidden between her legs.
                              Do I lack skill
As a rider? Am I too old? It could be, and her bucking
Makes me write a verse on her back with a red-hot poker.
Then she twists her body, swells her breasts and neighs,
Enlacing her eyes in the galloping, fleeing waters.

I'm eating her from inside and in my claw I clench
A place of impossible fruits. Knots of pleasure and howling—
Can you hear them? Today I met the mare of all my dreams,
She too is dying of love and I don't understand...

There's an Error in the Depths of the Glass

Someone is calling to me from inside my glass,
Cries that soak my nights with a brine in which I hear
Horsemen riding by.
Where are their faces? All they have are fixed
Masks of cruelty, that inverted love, that hole
Of hatred and silence.
Concerning Zedekiah it is written, 2 Kings 25:
"A breach having been made in the wall, they all fled
Into the deaf night but the soldiers caught them
And pronounced sentence against the King:
They killed his children in his sight and put a bitter
Spoon filled with vinegar to his lips;
They blinded him with hot coals, burning out his eyeballs,
Then they bound him in chains and led him off."
Why ask why? Today Babylon is everywhere.

                       In the depths of my glass at times I hear
Someone sobbing, and hands scrabbling at cold walls,
While I, among the feathers of my pillow, dream cruelty
Does not exist.
           That its demented root is dry at last.
                     Its blades in the air.

Nude Eating an Octopus

to Guy Borremans

Stretched between pearly iridescent folds of quartz,
She moves like a drumskin drifting on water.
She feels her sheets burn bit by bit, the eiderdown
Crumple into strata, tentacles fasten themselves to the warm
Surface of her body, groping for that live volcano at her root,
Sacrament bordered by snow between her legs.

She thinks the monster is taking her to the depths, to
      wound-abysses,
Falling slowly until it reaches vertigo: the rents and tears
That crisscross it and drink it empty, down to the secret
Acid of the holy mantis who, erect now, is cutting off
Its members one by one, weaving its tentacles into a delicate
Fabric, transparent in the fountain of splintered glass that makes it
      drunk,
Turning it into a knot that spills ink to the four
Quarters, not knowing why, or if by now it is only a frenzy
Of self-destruction under the caress of that kaleidoscope in the deep.

The woman is having a dream, the impossible desire to swallow the
      sea,
And the shadow of a meteor can be seen passing across her sheets.
Now, she says, I know thirst; I feel lewdness boiling in the bucket of
      the well.

Friends Are Dying, Vanishing into the Air

Friends are dying, vanishing into the air.
No warning, and then I can't talk with them except in dreams
Of things lost: the poem I carry folded in my wallet,
Photos of the girl we loved, who fell ill
Of loneliness, of being forgotten.
The one who took those pills
And on a rainy day we had to watch her dropping into a ditch
Like a withered branch down there in the mud.

Slow thorn, the rain knows crying.
Maybe there's one more day for us, one more bitter sun, to fight
The hours, to face down life. But it hurts that there may be.

Gone from the World, Born to Another Sun

Absence, the sound of insects out of hell
Buzzing down there in a dark dawn: Rosamel has died
And Thérèse, who always saved him, has fallen on the ice.
My parents are dead and I can't go see them, my brother
Carlos died, I'm afraid they buried him with his wooden leg,
The fate that changed his life forever.

Ida died, my passionate sister, and her family after her.
Trying to outface his destiny, Gómez-Correa died
And with him the ruined root of Mandrágora. Pellegrini died:
Aldo the good. Enrique Molina set sail, that doubting captain,
And I see my loves, flesh of my flesh, plunge down
The cataracts of the image.

   The caravan winds by, we're on our way to celebrate
Poetry on the other side, near the heart where all those absences,
Those wounds and wandering flames, are quenched.

Lounging Against a Night Stone

Lounging against a night stone, I watch time passing
In the retorts of the pit. What dragged us here?
Why are the far stars winking, exploding, going out?
Ringed in by shadow, I know I'm coal burning myself,
Grieving for lips I carry inside me, sketched on my bones.

Days and weeks go by and I don't manage to decode
The words on the wall, to read the signs in your heart,
The swell and fall of the wind there, your fate, queen
Of unbelievers who cannot see through masks.

Under a pious veil you set fire to the straps
Of pleasure bound all around us, the landscape that has no end
When you stretch out in bed and an eternal, limitless
Delight descends. Then why do the days close up sometimes
And darknesses that deafen all mercy fall?

Our ancestral star, the skin of the eclipse so long awaited, creaks.
We've reached the hurricane's still centre. Open your eyes.

I Have a Wound in My Memory

to Javier Guzmán

I've never been to Transylvania, never visited the castle
Of Vlad the Impaler, who survives down through the years
In everyone. I've never met him in my dreams,
Never marauded on the sheer cliffs of pallid skin where death,
The devoured one, the body with no eyelids, waits in ambush.

But I have beat on the walls and howled like a wolf at seeing
A pulse of tenderness and blood in the swan's white neck—
She that I can't forget, so beautiful, the one to whom they burnt
Petals and bone marrow, was all stupidity, all pleasure.

The world disappears and I'm alone forever once again,
Stretched out on a hospital bed. White birds peck me
And I feel a sun of blood spilling out, into probes, into flasks
Where no pleasure is. There's a wound in my memory.

I won't be back again, there's no key to the mystery
Of knife-edged teeth and the lips that sip human marrow.
What I'd like is to harpoon that ghost I glimpse in dreams
And grapple her to me, for only she could satisfy, My Lady
Fortuna, the wanderer, mistress of my death.

What Is Real Is Bitter

What is real is bitter, a place of red-hot, winking stones.
There I spent my childhood. Out on the desert you could see
A fountain, and a grove in whose branches azure birds
Shifted and flew, singing as they watched a mysterious boat
       pass by,
An enchanted city that sailed through dreams, that I looked for
On maps but it's not there, it's folded in the forgotten.

The days run on and cascades of images fall,
Ever-merging things and colours, gems of the torment
That never stops, though snow falls year by year,
Stooping my back. With words I make a net
That might restore the ocean, bring us back
Music's magic, as when someone grieves in his bonds
And a butterfly poses its splendor on the spilled-out crying.

The real is bitter, my black beetle burrows underground,
The lost things won't come again.
                 What's left is water running
Over our face, cleansing us within as in the past,
And me, standing on the long-gone balcony, seeing her wave
From the ghost ship gently rocking in a swarm
Of petals and foam. If you don't love me anymore, say so,
I shout into the gusty wind that beats me. My stigmata
Form the letters of your name. This is no dream.

The Snake Eaters

From Matehuala south: desert scalding in a bath of brine
And at the roadside swarms of women who beg for alms
Never received.
        Among the yuccas, a cane, and hanging from its tip
The remains of a snake, an empty skin, and on the ground,
Poised on one foot, flesh-eater, a hawk behind its eye of steel.

Alone and wretched: almost mute they beg for someone
To change their lives, carry them past that horizon
Where day by day the hawk harries the serpent: there is only
Rancid bread, milk full of salt, to drown thirst, murder hunger.

You who put them in the desert, why don't you give them
Water? Why always the spectacle of that steel beak
Slitting snakes open from end to end? And why
Those children begging, useless, unable even to dream?

It's true then that this is where hell opens and burns
Insects in madness. I summon up my childhood, where I was happy,
But it hurts now in the depths, in memory, to repeat those images.
There's no way out. Suddenly the skies are closed.

Fire Swallower

We stepped on the brakes. Red light. The night
Is a wet cloth stretched out in front of
This metal being that bellows and sings
Like the sirens we've forgotten about so long.

A man jumps out and shouts with mute gesticulations:
Wait, stop the world, quit making so much noise!
In his hand there's a flame and in his mouth the knot
That alcohol ties as tight as a knife blade, the food
Of threats, and now it slashes farther, flashing
In the thousand tongues crushed inside his burnt lips,
And he smiles...
        Is life nothing but spare change anymore?
Something hurts in the pit of that fugitive star,
Someone orders you: Stop!

    But we eased off the brakes and, Let's get out of here.
The night was unremitting. The light was green.

Man Plowing His Field

Bent following the blade his ox drags,
He opens his earth's warm lips and traces its furrows
In an act of love, dropping his seed,
Covering it with clay and longing, giving it flesh in dreams.

So day by day he comes to hear the sounds
The maize makes budding in the dark, opening
A channel, rising in upward cataracts, seeking
The sun's skin, the caress that lets it breathe,
Grow into leaves and achieve the solidity of the stalk.

I see you and my eyes don't grasp the mystery.
Above your happiness fly the *zanates*, singing
From their blackness, and the field herons that come
To look for worms, to scratch in the happiness of being here,
Being just parts of a summer that flows away:
The silence of nature blesses you, the gift
Of life that is scarcely a breeze and is eternal.

The rain, ancient canticle, will come and the wind
Will soothe the lightning that burns the night, and you
Teach yourself hope, to talk with seeds, to travel
With the moon among the sprouts, to live wandering
In leaves that hug you, seek you, encircle you.

Here we are, brother, for a million ages
We watched the jacaranda grow, the perfume of its flowers
Pierced us and in the age of love there came forth
A song of celebration, a music like copal smoke,
Life that, in us, is the footsteps of a proverb.

Will we too one day be growing in the dark?
Will destiny, like you there on your furrows, listen
To our call that gropes, that quests for the star of warmth,
Of sweetness? Are you listening for how these things will be?

Here it comes now, falling on us, descending gently
Disguised as tears, the rain.

Zapotec Weaver

to my friend Lucio Aquino Cruz
of Santa Ana del Valle, Oaxaca

I was formed on this loom, from before time my bones were its frame,
I feel its animal graze in my marrow and bleat, shrouded in cold.
Millennia ago I wove all that. Life carded the wool inside me,
Dividing it into threads the way a woman's fingers divide the mist.

And this, my time, belongs to the Other. Years go by like water.
Before my earliest ancestor hums destiny's repeating weft.
Colours open, colours close around me and the tapestry extends
    itself
Like a river in all directions, a dream without an end.

My mother wove: I saw, and nursed from her the thread my wife
    weaves
Day after day now through implacable seasons that fold us over,
Bend us toward dust, and erode us: multiplied into children,
Love's outcry sets fire to a closed horizon of narrow alleyways.

Walls of warm adobe, my days constructed of bitter sweetness.
And they call out—I hear them—to sleepers lost in the night
Of the weaver. Sometimes his colours hold warm fruits, scents of other
    worlds,
Pulverized insects, or rose-coloured bark the years have pitted and
    scored.

Existence repeats itself in us as figures, rhombs, fretted borders,
And a phantom shuttle moves through them: a shuttle I can't hear,
One that my hands don't drive, but I know that it is time,
The secret design, which in due course will incorporate my death.

144

And if at last we are only a dark skein's unwinding,
Will a door ever open for the suns wandering in my blood,
The swarm of petals that is God and all my children,
Twilight-skinned weavers of the cup we drink in tears?

Between warp and woof, my destiny: invisible faces
Of the unknown future, which is only a tangle of roots
Singing in the earth, which is eternal.

The Glyph for Destiny

Because we only come to sing to the face
Of the phantasm that glides away in a thousand mirrors,
Skin that reduplicates itself, eyes that study us
From behind the pitchers on the table, the colour in our
    brushstrokes,
Nothing but scars on stone, traces of the burin,
Remainders of blood, saliva, the desire
That persists in those who imagined
The impossible...

            And here we are. Ephemerids
For having seen that the spirit endures and changes
To a cry. Petals that sketch the invisible flower
Of going on.

                From stone to stone the echo, and from woman
To man the shape of the flame that burns inside us,
Carried downstream toward the deep (I can hear
The waterfall's roar) where life sounds in the vaults
Of conch shells...going on, passing through an instant
That makes us homesick for all eternity.

Female Skull Decorated with Turquoises

(Tomb VII, Monte Albán, Mixtec culture)

Is it you, this beauty, this woman who there, in time,
Sings and repeats the miracle of existing, of being only once?
Flower of grace, your eyes pierce mine
And with your lips I extinguish the thirst of many lives
When night falls and you pour out your skin, when the black stone
Falls between your shoulders, and is perfume, and is dream.

Talk to me flower of desire, petals of lives past,
Moons that burnt our momentary bodies,
The secret language of lovers, ferocious desire
To drink each other and be fixed in an ecstasy
Without yesterday or tomorrow, only the quiet
Lightning of being dust dragged by the wind.

Will that time come back and establish itself once more,
Will you return, bird that passes like a melody?
Will we come again to feel the hope, the language of fire
That burnishes us within, to demand the impossible, be eternal?
In the whirl of passion, whispers, dreams,
Are we just images the wind plays on the sand?

And now here you are, fragments of turquoise encrusting your face,
Your lips can't caress the honey of words and someone
Has put in your eyes the shells that tides throw on the beach.
If only I could kiss you, could reach into your marrow
And understand you are still the same poppy of fire
I once held in these hands, head of the goddess, enigma.

A Garden in Huayapan

We were looking for a place and in a pond we saw
Two snakes copulating. There was a machete-hacked
Jacaranda and two pits so deep they seemed to me the bilges
Of the huge ship we all work. For years the people had extracted
Bricks from this earth, knotting the clay, burning it in fire.

Was this the spot where we could still our lives? Susana
Insisted, day after day, wanting it here, the house we'd dreamed.
From Puebla we brought in a couple hundred small trees.
We opened a well: there was water there, reflecting the moon.

Today I see a *pirul*: this tree we planted recalls my old ones,
Hundreds of birds hit the windows, exclaiming, mad
With love, and flowers grow. Who granted us all this?
The woman: she gives us back a part of childhood.

Bees Against the Window

Sometimes that buzzing of wings surprises me,
The rumour of destiny that impels words,
Conjuring the music that has to save the soul
From the body's clay.
       Then I turn, start to dig
In yellowing papers, find no way out,
question by means of images that maybe don't exist,
listen again to the fever in colours,
The eyes that watch me, the ones I've hunted
For centuries through burning woods.

Is there an invisible thread, a harmony that comes
From the skin of your wings? Your tears
Evoke a perfume now grown strange.
         Will we return
To our deciphering the music of the word, our listening
To swallow the rivers that flow across the skies in the night?
The wall is bricked up, blank, solid with questions.
If you'd listen to the petals of dream, you'd have your reply.

Monte Albán, Sacred Mountain

I coursed through half the world and came to this:
I can open my window and see there in the distance
The Holy Mountain, Danibaan, with its perfect plaza
Half disclosing every day under the sun
The enigmas humans created to prove that they exist,
That there is a reason for being—to exalt the spirit.

Here through millennia live the generations
Of the people of the clouds, whose language is the music of words,
The ones who created that vast plaza on the heights
To sing and celebrate their vision of earth.

Whoever makes it here can see how fragile and small,
A flower losing its petals, the human is, but in harmony
How it grows and multiplies. The palaces
Follow each other down the edge of a vast esplanade
And the squares dance and rise.

        Enigmatic blocks of stone that guard
The granite silence and nonetheless move
Something in us: the hope of knowing it's possible
To try the impossible, follow a star's path down the millennia,
The swarm of lights that carries us.

The builders here: what did they live? What desires,
Passions, and visions took shape in their days?
        We're fragile,
We decorate in stone and are unmade in dust.
As the poet said, the quetzal's feathers are minuscule petals,
They move us, but no one knows what inwardly they are.
Perhaps the Life Giver is dreaming in us. But silence falls.

A Bunch of Carnations

An old woman peddling a bunch of carnations
Kept following me. No, I told her. Where would I put them?
She held out her palm and looked me in the eyes.
They're twenty pesos, she said, they're very beautiful.
Maybe you'd enjoy them—maybe you need them.
I gave them to the next female acquaintance I happened to see
And I told her that they had blossomed just for her.

I can't say exactly why I wrote these lines
About the flowers of letters, the calligrams, which follow me
Down my long life and keep lighting the signs that love
And friendship do exist, that I believe. But here they are.
Maybe you'll enjoy them—maybe you need them, like me.

Adorable Ladies, and Pervertible, Perhaps

They undulate by, leaving just a wake,
A cordon of incense, the forbidden
Image of a gaze into the depths,
Of sewing the lips to the tongue, stitch
By sharp stitch, of failing to hear the music
That cascades from their warm breasts
Into nothingness while they smile, disquieted,
Watching the sun, applying makeup, chatting.

They've always been there, marble ladies,
Chatelaines of illusion, sensual, chaste,
Whose eyes half open when the Prophet passes.
Virtuous, crossing themselves, they don't want to hear
The syllables that gnaw their lips. They shake,
Not knowing why tortures follow them, hunting them.

Maybe they're sleeping. Why are they denied
The happiness of seeing themselves? Caressed
By the wings of evening, adorable vestals, the temptation
Of Being in their throats, they dance, hidden, not knowing
The miracle is eternal. They gather honey in their hips
And stand there, waiting in front of the closed moons
Of mirrors. Untouchable by mortals.
                    Who could nail them down and spread
Them open on arms of wood? Set their marrow
On fire, wake them up and make them feel the sea,
The dust of love, the cries in which they wash their hair?

Adorable, attractive ladies—and pervertible, let it be.

Perfume of Memory

The birds returned today—I heard their voices
Pecking in the blue patio of my spirit.
Many nights they'd flown over the emerald as large as a fruit,
Earth, where dust spins its rings.

But now those pilgrims are here, with the absent air
Of people just arrived from the paradises you rule
With the honey of your gaze, taking good care
Of an invisible swarm that drinks the perfume of dreams in you.

Can a few letters set the rose without thorns
In the magic of a name? I recall my mother, my childhood
In the oasis where mirages nested, plumes of illusion.
For you, Dove, my heart holds a drop of warm amber,
You who deep in my eyes are the river I saw flowing as a boy,
Enchantment of the perfume of your breasts, breasts of an idol.

This linking of words to words on a destiny we know
Nothing about, that I invoke in you...as if, standing by the
            ancient ocean
As it created your lips, its shores, I heard distant shells
Singing, and the song was the foam that licks you from within...

Maybe you're near, it's your desperate steps I hear on the stairs.
Blind now, we half make out appearances, that's all,
Never the invisible, the shadow behind each leaf,
Fugitive image I remember when I see birds fly.

ACKNOWLEDGEMENTS

Special acknowledgement is gladly paid to the Banff International Literary Translation Centre, and to its first director and current faculty member Linda Gaboriau. Sr. Zeller, his wife Susana Wald, and I were invited to be participants in the inaugural session of the BILTC in August 2003. In the ideal circumstances of that residency, some of these translations were made, many others were revised from earlier versions, and the concept and outline of *The Rules of the Game: Selected Shorter Poems of Ludwig Zeller* were established.

Most of these translations are based on earlier versions which I did in collaboration with Theresa Moritz, Susana Wald, and Beatriz Hausner, and with the advice of Sr. Zeller on many difficulties. My thanks to them, and to the publishers of the books in which the earlier versions appeared: Mosaic Press, Oakville, Ontario, for *Ludwig Zeller in the Country of the Antipodes: Poems 1964-1979* (1979), *The Marble Head and Other Poems* (1986), and *The Ghost's Tattoos* (1989); Exile Editions, Toronto, Ontario, for *To Saw the Belovèd to Pieces Only When Necessary* (1990); and Ekstasis Editions, Victoria, British Columbia, for *Body of Insomnia* (1996) and *The Eye on Fire* (2007). A version of my translation of "The Elements" was published in *The Malahat Review*. The first version of "On a Photograph of Ezra Pound" was presented as a handmade chapbook by Nicky Drumbolis under one of his Letters imprints, *On a Photograph of Ezra Pound / Sobre una fotografía de Ezra Pound* (Toronto: twobitter forty-eight, 1994). Twenty earlier versions of translations on their way toward *The Rules of the Game* were published by Luciano Iacobelli as a handmade book, *The Snake Eaters* (Toronto: Lyricalmyrical Handmades, n.d.).

The text used for most of the translations is that of Ludwig Zeller's complete poems through 1996, *Los engranajes del encantamiento* (Mexico City: Universidad Nacional Autónoma de México, Consejo Nacional para la Cultura y las Artes, y Editorial Aldus; 1996). The text for the remaining volumes is that of the first Spanish editions: *Imágenes en el ojo llameante* (Toronto: Artifact, 1999); *El embrujo de México* (Morelia: Universidad Michoacana de San Nicolás de Hidalgo, 2003); *Piel de los delirios* (Villahermosa, Tabasco: Gatsby, 2008). Grateful acknowledgement is made to the Mexican poet and publisher Juan Escareño, who produced the Spanish original of *The Eye on Fire*, *Imágenes en el ojo llameante*, as a handmade and an online book under his Artifact imprint. In the case of this book, the translations incorporate some changes made by Sr. Zeller subsequent to the Artifact edition and found in the Spanish text of the bilingual Ekstasis edition.